The
Loan Arranger
Guide

A no nonsense guide to understanding the
lending process, products and their features,
so you the consumer, can get the best deal!

Andrew Brien

To my wife and children.

Contents

• •

Acknowledgments

. . . .

I would like to acknowledge the assistance I have received over the years from my colleagues in the finance industry, including Brian, Harri, Phil, Sally, Peter, Ross, and Mike. Your support over the years has been invaluable.

Introduction

Australia has one of the world's most competitive lending industries, offering you genuine choice. The lending industry is wide-ranging, including major banks, branchless banks, regional banks, building societies, non-bank lenders, and credit unions, providing a massive number of different loans to individuals and businesses.

This book is aimed at consumers. You don't need to understand the lending industry to benefit from this book.

Having an understanding about this complex industry can help you:

- Save money by getting a better deal
- Save time by not stumbling through the loan application process
- Access better lending products that offer you the opportunity to build your wealth
- Know what your legal rights are and what you should do if you find yourself in trouble
- Understand mortgage brokers
- Know what to expect after you take out a loan

- Understand what loan features are available and what they offer you
- Make sure you get the flexibility you need without paying for what you don't need

Getting and repaying a home loan is a major part of the average person's life. Loan terms available now are generally thirty years or greater. It's often the biggest financial commitment you will make; you will most likely still be repaying your home loan well into your working life, and in some cases after.

Understanding the complex market is not easy; such a wide choice of different loan products can at times make a decision harder. This book has been developed to assist you in understanding, at a basic level, the process of getting a home loan.

While the industry is complicated, the majority of lenders follow a similar path to approve a loan. There is a lot you can do to improve your chances of getting the best loan possible.

A basic understanding of the application process will save you time and money when looking for a new loan. An understanding of the fees, both initial and ongoing, can assist in the decision-making process. The loan with the lowest interest rate may not be the best loan in the long term.

It's also a good idea to know what will happen after you get the loan. The costs and consequences of the choices you make now will have an impact in years to come. For example, will you be moving in two to three years? If you were to choose a five-year fixed rate, you may be faced with an expensive break rate fee.

The Australian Bureau of Statistics estimates the total Australian residential lending market in 2008–09 at $1.75 trillion. Lending in Australia is big business![1]

Getting the best deal may take some time, but it's worth it. I strongly recommend that before you enter into any loan, you should seek independent financial and legal advice.

If you have chosen to use the services of a mortgage broker, think about getting a second opinion from a different mortgage broker or

---

1 Year Book Australia, 2009-10 – Lending by Financial Institutions

your bank, and call the lender directly to see if you are getting the best deal.

There are, of course, a few things that you should really understand, and throughout the book I will attempt to answer these key questions:

1. Should you do a do-it-yourself (DIY) search or use a mortgage broker to find your next home loan?
2. How do you get approved fast and without hassles?
3. What loan should you get, including looking at variable rate vs. fixed rate options?

Quick lessons, tips, and warnings used in this book

To help you get the most out of this book, I have attempted to provide you with quick lessons, such as pros and cons, tips, and warnings here and there to highlight important points. Here's what each type aims to provide you with:

💣 **WARNING:** Pay extra attention when you see the "warning" symbol. It means you may be about to do something or forget to do something that you will regret later.

🖋 **TIP:** When you see the "tip" symbol, I'm providing you with basic tips or lists to make the task discussed simpler to complete.

👍 **PROS and** 👎 **CONS:** A simple list of pros, reasons for doing the action; and cons, reasons for not doing the action.

⚖ **LEGAL ISSUES:** When you see the "legal issues" symbol, I'm providing information on the legal environment, including relevant acts of government. It's important that you know your rights and any issues you may face.

"Yes, I can help you with your loan
questions. I'm the loan arranger."

Chapter 1:

Before you start looking
for a new home loan

In this Chapter:

➤ DIY home loan searches
➤ Using a mortgage broker
➤ How much do you need to borrow?
➤ Is there any time when you should not refinance or apply for a new loan?
➤ Government grants and incentives

Starting the Search

So you need a new home loan. Have you found your dream home? Do you need to refinance your existing loan? Either way, you will need to search for a new loan and potentially a new lender. This can be time-consuming. There are thousands of loan products out there, from hundreds of lenders.

Do you really know what you need? How will you find the right mix of interest rate and features? What are the latest trends? Which lenders are looking for your business and willing to make it worth your while to go with them?

These are just some of the questions you are likely to have. But there is a simpler question you need to ask: do you want to do it yourself or go to a mortgage broker?

Do you love to research stuff? Have you got a lot of time? Are you financially literate? If so, you may want to do a DIY search.

Are you pressed for time? Do you just want someone to give you a range of options? Do you need to talk face-to-face with someone? Does going to a one-stop shop where you can see a selection of options interest you? If so, you should consider using a mortgage broker.

DIY Home Loan Search

Thankfully, today you don't have to arrange a meeting during business hours at the lender's office to discuss your home loan. Back in the 1980s, you almost had to go on your hands and knees when seeing the bank manager! Today you can surf the Net and get the basic information (interest rates, application fees, and ongoing fees) from almost any lender's website. There are even a few comparison sites that provide thousands of products at the click of a button.

However, to get an idea of the credit requirements you will need to contact the lender. This may be in person at a branch, or over the phone or Internet. A few lenders still have "mobile managers" who are able to visit you at your home or office.

To really confirm how much a lender will allow you to borrow requires some basic information about your financial history and employment. The lender can then estimate the maximum loan amount they can give you and discuss products with you.

🔥 **WARNING:** Don't apply (complete an application form or agree to a credit check) at each lender, as each application will be recorded on your credit file. This can backfire on you, making it difficult to get a loan. Lenders don't like to see a lot of enquiries on your credit report.

Comparing different lenders may seem simple, but you need to understand what's important to you as a borrower first. Below is my list of suggested key items to compare:

1. Interest rate
2. Entry fees
3. Ongoing fees
4. Product features
5. Communication methods

There are few tools out there to assist you in comparing different lenders. Your best option is to ask set questions; that way you can compare answers. For example, you could ask questions about communication methods: Does the lender have an after-hours call centre? Branches close to your work so you can get there at lunch time?

For a DIY home loan search, here's how I recommend choosing the lenders to contact:

- Start with your existing bank/lender
- Ask family and friends who are happy with their lenders
- Find out if your employer has a relationship with a lender and if you might get any discounts from this relationship
- Don't forget to look at ads. There may be a special offer out there!

✏️ **TIP:** You should start by contacting your existing bank/lender. They will at least have a relationship with you, so they should be quickest in providing some indication of a maximum loan amount and recommending a product.

Pros and Cons of a DIY Loan Search

As with anything, there are positives and negatives, and deciding to start a DIY loan search has some important positives and negatives.

👍 PROS

- You may be able to access special offers that are direct to the public
- You can take your time and ask questions
- No conflict of interest

👎 CONS

- Time-consuming
- Difficult to accurately compare offers
- You will only have access to lenders you know about

Generally, unless you have a lot of time and are financially literate, a DIY loan search is going to be time-consuming and may not result in you getting the best loan for your needs.

There is an alternative!

Mortgage Brokers

Mortgage brokers are experts providing qualified, independent advice on loans and financial products from a range of different lenders.

The industry has matured considerably in recent years through a combination of regulation and competition. Generally, the days of "cowboy" brokers are over.

Mortgage brokers must comply with a number of legislative requirements including the National Consumer Credit Protection Act (NCCP), the Anti-Money Laundering and Counter-Terrorism Financing Act, the Fair Trading Act, and others.

The NCCP places a number of obligations on mortgage brokers recommending a loan to you. Basically, they must:
- Not recommend an unsuitable loan to you
- Make enquiries about your requirements and objectives

- Confirm your financial situation
- Verify information in assessing whether a loan is unsuitable for you

The NCCP requires the mortgage broker to define a loan as unsuitable if:

- You could not repay the loan
- Repaying the loan would cause you financial hardship
- The loan does not meet your financial objectives

This new requirement means mortgage brokers have to justify their recommendations in detail.

While the mortgage brokering industry is not currently directly regulated, there are two industry self-regulatory bodies, the Mortgage & Finance Association of Australia (MFAA) and the Finance Brokers Association of Australia (FBAA). Mortgage brokers who are members of these associations have met minimum qualifications and have some experience in the industry.

Mortgage broker services are generally provided to you at no cost; the mortgage broker will receive a commission from the lender for introducing the business. This commission is made up of two separate payments. The first is an upfront payment paid when the loan settles. The second is an ongoing or "trail" payment made as long as the loan remains with that lender. We may see in the future a change towards brokers charging a fee directly to you.

Mortgage brokers are often very flexible, being willing to offer you a range of alternatives, not just a single choice. In the past, mortgage brokers tended to deal with customers who had special requirements that made arranging their loans more complicated. Meanwhile, the banks' branches seemed more and more like fast food outlets, where you were sometimes asked if you would like a home loan with your deposit! However, everyone now seems time-poor, and the mortgage broker model of offering a wide choice of loans from a single source is very appealing.

For consumers, mortgage brokers offer the opportunity to review a number of loan options from a number of different lenders.

Finance Broking Contracts

In New South Wales, mortgage brokers must obtain a signed finance broking contract prior to starting work for you. This is a legal document that sets out:

- Your contact details
- The amount of credit to be obtained
- The term of the loan
- The maximum payment you are prepared to make
- The maximum interest rate you are prepared to pay
- Details of each lender on the broker panel
- The name and address of the broker
- The amount of commission payable by you

Mortgage brokers *must* provide you with a finance broking contract. The only exception is when the mortgage broker only offers loans from a single lender. New disclosure requirements will result in you being provided with three documents; a credit guide, a quote and a credit proposal disclosure.

What to look for in a Mortgage Broker

When you meet the mortgage broker, remember you are looking for an excellent communicator and an expert who understands dozens of different lending policies. The mortgage broker needs to pay attention to details to truly be able to offer constructive advice. Look for a mortgage broker with knowledge of the lending industry, including the legislative requirements, the legal aspects of lending (purchasing or refinancing properties), the tax aspects of investing in real estate, and the approval and settlement processes.

Mortgage Broker Checklist

To ensure you get the best out of your relationship with a mortgage broker, you should at the very least ask some basic questions:

1. Which lenders do you deal with?

   Does the mortgage broker offer real choice? The lenders should be a spread of banks, credit unions and non-bank lenders.

2. Does the mortgage broker have interest rate comparison sheets, and key facts sheets for all the loans offered?

   They allow you to review each loan product using the same benchmark loan amounts and terms.

3. How does the mortgage broker get paid?

   Generally, all mortgage brokers get a commission from the lender. The amount of this commission should be disclosed to you in a finance broking contract, and you should consider whether the recommendation is based on your needs and not on the commission payable.

4. How is the comparison made between loan products?

   This is critical. The mortgage broker should talk about interest rates, entry and exit fees, loan features, and the differences in credit policies for each lender. If not, are they really offering you advice?

5. Is the mortgage broker a member of an industry group?

   Dealing with a mortgage broker who is a member of an industry group adds protection and a formal complaint-handling procedure.

6. What professional qualification does the mortgage broker have? What experience do they have?

   Are you dealing with a qualified mortgage broker who is experienced, or someone who just started last week? The industry standard qualification is a Certificate IV in Financial Services. You can ask to speak to existing or past clients to check on how the mortgage broker acted in the past.

7. Does the mortgage broker have professional indemnity insurance?

This further protects you as a consumer. Mortgage brokers without this insurance will not be able to submit your loan application to most lenders. Don't deal with uninsured mortgage brokers.

8. Who will complete the credit check?

   It's important to understand if the mortgage broker will submit your application to multiple lenders, as each lender may complete a credit check. This can be damaging to your credit file history if you have numerous recent enquiries.

9. Will the mortgage broker be able to assist you after the application is approved?

   Mortgage brokers should be prepared to assist you after approval, and even after settlement of your loan, so if you get the message that you will be dealing with the lender, not the broker, beware!

10. If the mortgage broker has a limited panel of lenders, or possibly only one lender, why is this?

    As a consumer, you need to understand why the mortgage broker has made such a decision, and whether what is on offer fits with what you are looking for in a lending product.

Complaints Procedures

Mortgage brokers must have a dispute-resolution procedure for handling complaints fairly. Mortgage brokers who are members of an industry body such as the MFAA will be able to provide access to a dispute-resolution scheme. This means you know the mortgage broker should be able to manage a complaint, including the recording of the complaint. You should get a written response, including a formal complaint form and an explanation of the investigation and resolution processes.

✍ **TIP:** Check the MFAA and FBAA websites to ensure your mortgage broker is really accredited.

Example organisations: complaints can be made directly to the following organisations regarding their members:

Mortgage & Finance Association of Australia (MFAA)

Finance Brokers Association of Australia (FBAA)

Pros and Cons of Using a Mortgage Broker

Using a mortgage broker to find your next loan can save you time and provide you with real choice. However, as with anything, there are positives and negatives.

☝ PROS

- They are usually free of charge and carry no obligation.
- They will often meet with you at a time and place that suits you, including over the telephone, by e-mail, or on the Internet.
- Most mortgage brokers will have access to a high number of lenders and products, offering you a comparison of suitable loans.
- Mortgage brokers have access to loan-comparison software that can quickly select a short list of loans that meet your key requirements.
- Some broker groups offer a flat commission to their mortgage brokers regardless of the lender selected, so the mortgage broker is not motivated by higher commissions.
- Some lenders offer special rates and products only to the broker market.
- Mortgage brokers have an understanding of the lender's credit policy and will not place you with a lender they believe will not approve your loan.

☝ CONS

- Mortgage brokers are paid on commission, so the bigger the loan, the more commission they get.

- Lenders often offer promotions to mortgage brokers to attract additional business volume. Will you be getting the best loan on offer, or the flavour of the month?

- Mortgage brokers are often blocked by lenders from submitting deals to your existing lender. The lenders see the customers as belonging to them and will not allow the mortgage broker to offer different loans, forcing the mortgage broker to offer loans from a different lender.

In general, mortgage brokers offer a good service that benefits both you and the lender. You should always compare offerings, but don't apply at multiple mortgage brokers or lenders, as this could damage your credit file.

SUMMARY: I've completed DIY loan searches in the past, and in general I've had no problems, but I'm an industry insider. When I last refinanced my home loan, I did contact a mortgage broker to discuss products I was aware of. The broker provided me with valuable information on exit fees that helped me decide on a lender.

I realize I've grown time-poor over the last few years, and mortgage brokers offer me the opportunity to quickly confirm what lenders and loans would suit me. Even as an industry insider, I truly believe mortgage brokers offer me more choice more quickly than I could find myself with a DIY search.

How Much Do You Need to Borrow?

It may seem like a silly question, but you do need to know how much you want to borrow.

If you are purchasing your first home you will need to cover the purchase price of the property plus any fees and costs. If you are refinancing you will need to repay the existing loan, including fees and the new lenders fees along with any costs.

Purchase Price – Deposit + Fees + Costs = Loan Amount

Fees include the application fee, the valuation fee, and Lender's Mortgage Insurance (LMI) if applicable. Costs include rates or strata fees already prepaid at settlement, and government charges such as transfer stamp duty, and registration fees.

Let's look at an example:

John and Mary are purchasing a new home in NSW for $585,000. They have a 10 percent deposit of $58,500 and have $50,000 in additional savings. How much will they need?

Purchase Price	$585,000
NSW Stamp Duty	$21,815
Legal Fees	$1,780
Council Rates and Water Rates (Payable to the seller for the per-paid rates)	$325
Loan Application Fee	$400
Lenders Mortgage Insurance Fee (LMI)	$6,500
Total Required for Settlement	**$615,820**
Less	
Deposit Paid	$58,500
Savings to be used for purchase	$50,000
Loan Amount Required	**$507,320**

If John and Mary were first-time home buyers, they would pay a reduced transfer stamp duty and receive the First Home Owner Grant of $7,000. It's important to understand that fees and costs can be substantial—in this case, over $30,000!

Are There Times When You Should Not Apply for a New Loan or Refinance?

There are a few times you should not look to apply for a new loan, as the lender is likely to decline your application.

When you have a new job. Lenders like to see stable employment, and having a new job, unless it's in the same industry, looks bad. You should really be in the job for at least six months before applying for a loan.

When you are in arrears. If you are in arrears and are attempting to refinance, the new lender will ask for evidence of your repayment history. When the new lender sees missed payments or over-limit arrears, they will likely decline the application. If you can't manage to pay your existing loans, how will you pay the new loan?

When your property is under construction or major renovation. Lenders don't like taking partly finished properties as security. The main reason is that if you fall into arrears and they have to foreclose and sell your property, it may be difficult to find someone willing to buy and finish the property.

Government Grants and Incentives

Federal, state, and territory governments offer incentives and grants for first-home owners in an effort to increase home affordability, which is currently at record lows.

These incentives fall into three groups:
1. Grants
2. Reduced transfer stamp duty
3. First home owner savings accounts

Grants

The First Home Owner Grant (FHOG) scheme was introduced in 2000 to offset the effect of the Goods and Services Tax (GST) on home ownership. It's a national scheme funded by the states and territories and administered under their own legislation.

Under the scheme, a one-off grant of $7,000 is payable to eligible first-home owners.

To be eligible, you must be an Australian citizen or permanent resident who has not owned a property in any Australian state or territory. There are also limits on the maximum value of the property you are purchasing, so in NSW the grant is not available to people purchasing a property worth more than $835,000.

If the home is purchased jointly, neither partner can have owned property before. The property must be used as your permanent residency within the first six months of the purchase and for a minimum period of one year. And yes, they do check up on you!

Reduced Transfer/Conveyancing Stamp Duty

The stamp duty or conveyancing duty cuts are designed to help first-home owners enter the property market.

New South Wales

First-home buyers receive a total exemption from conveyancing duty for metropolitan property values of up to $500,000, with a partial exemption phasing out at $600,000. The State Government has recently announced that this exemption will be removed and replaced with an exemption only available on newly constructed properties from 2012.

For vacant land, the threshold value for full duty exemption is $300,000, with a partial exemption applying up to $450,000.

Victoria

For purchases with a settlement date on or after 1 July 2011, conveyancing duty will be reduced for eligible first-home buyers purchasing a residence valued up to $600,000. To be eligible for the conveyancing duty reduction, you must have received or be entitled to receive the First Home Owner Grant and must also live in the property for twelve months commencing within twelve months of settlement.

The conveyancing duty reduction of 50 percent will be phased in over four years, with a 20 percent reduction on 1 July 2011, followed by additional 10 percent reductions on 1 January 2013, 1 January 2014, and 1 September 2014.

Queensland

No conveyancing duty applies to first home purchases of up to $500,000, with a partial exemption phasing out at $594,999.

Vacant land receives a full exemption for purchases up to $250,000, with a partial exemption phasing out at $399,999.

Western Australia

First-home buyers receive a total exemption from conveyancing duty for metropolitan property values of up to $500,000, with a partial exemption phasing out at $600,000.

For vacant land, the threshold value for full duty exemption is $300,000, with a partial exemption applying up to $400,000.

Australian Capital Territory

Eligible first-home buyers are charged minimum conveyancing duty for properties up to $360,000. For properties valued above $360,000, new buyers are charged a rate of $20.55 for each $100 or part thereof up to $445,000, with no concession thereafter.

For vacant land, there is a lower threshold value of $200,500, with a rate of $16.20 for each $100 or part thereof up to $246,100, with no concession above this.

A household income threshold of $100,000 per annum applies, with an allowance for children of $3,300 per child.

Tasmania

Conveyancing duty relief of up to $4,000 is available for first-home buyers purchasing a property up to a value of $350,000.

No concession applies for properties above $350,000.

A refund of conveyancing duty of up to $2,400 is available to first-home owners who have purchased and built on land after 2004. The refund is payable on land with a dutiable value of up to $175,000, and is paid on the completion of the construction of the home.

South Australia

For properties where the sale and purchase contract is entered into on or after 27 May 2004 and prior to 5 June 2008, first-home purchases up to $80,500 will receive a full concession.

For first-home purchases where the property is valued between $80,501 and $100,000, the concession will reduce from 100 percent to 50 percent (2.5 percent reduction per $1,000 of property value) and will remain at 50 percent where the property is valued between $100,001 and $150,000.

Thereafter, the concession reduces by $24 for every $1000 increase in property value above $150,000, and it phases out completely for first-home purchases above $250,000.

Northern Territory

All first-home buyers receive a conveyancing duty concession on the first $540,000 up to a maximum concession of $26,730.

First Home Saver Accounts

First Home Saver Accounts (FHSAs) are a simple, tax-effective way to save for your first home through a combination of government contributions and low taxes. Contributions can be made by you or another party, such as an employer. The government will make additional contributions, which will be paid directly into your account, after you have filed your tax return.

The government will contribute 17 percent on the first $5,000 (indexed for inflation) of individual contributions made each year. Interest will be taxed at a rate of 15 percent.

There is a limit of $75,000 (indexed for inflation) on the overall account balance.

To be eligible, you must be at least eighteen years old and under sixty-five years old, and you must not have previously purchased or built a home to live in.

To withdraw funds, a minimum contribution of $1,000 is needed to be made over the course of at least four years.

State Lending Programs

State governments have been providing lending programs since the early 1960s. South Australia and Western Australia are the only states remaining still able to provide regular home loans to the public in their states. In both cases, the programs (HomeStart in SA and Key-Start in WA) are designed to assist low-income borrowers or state housing tenants into affordable housing.

Generally, the loans offered are similar to retail lending products but are discounted or include interest-free components. They often support local programs to build houses or support indigenous communities.

New South Wales and Victoria have programs that are very small and generally lend to existing borrowers only.

SUMMARY: Government grants and incentives can quickly add up. If you are a first-home buyer, contact your local Office of State Revenue for details of grants and incentives on offer.

Chapter 2:

Comparing lenders and key loan features

● ●

In this Chapter:

➤ How to compare lenders
➤ A guide to lenders
➤ Are you rate-sensitive?
➤ Should You fix?
➤ Basic or full-featured loan: which should you go with?

● ●

Having decided how much you want to borrow and how you will search for a new lender, it's time to consider the different types of lenders.

In Australia there is a wide range of financial institutions able to offer loans. It is important to understand the differences between them and what they can offer. You should also know that your lender will be your partner in home ownership for a long time.

How to Compare Lenders

How do you compare different lenders? The usual way is to compare the three key requirements: communication, fees, and rates.

Communication

How do you want to contact your lender? How will you manage your loan? If you want to go to see a manager and need a branch to deposit funds, then you will avoid the branchless banks and some of the non-bank lenders and head for the traditional major banks, credit unions, and building societies.

However, if you are content to use Internet banking and telephone your lender about more detailed issues, then almost any lender will meet your needs. Most lenders have call centres that operate after hours and on weekends.

Fees

Fees should include the costs of establishing the new loan, not just the ongoing costs! Recent changes by the federal government mean exit fees are now banned, so there is one less thing you need to consider. Like telcos, the major lenders now bundle services such as loans, transactional accounts, credit cards, and insurance. Look for low fees or a reasonable bundle. My current package has an annual fee of $300. For that I get a 0.70 percent reduction on my variable interest rate, no annual fee on my credit card, and a discount on my insurance.

Rates

The interest rate will of course be an important consideration, but remember: low interest rate loans often have few features and hefty fees for upgrades!

✎**TIP:** If you already have a bank account with a lender, you should contact them first, or ask your mortgage broker about their offerings. As your existing lender already has a relationship with you they may be able to approve your loan faster.

A Guide to Lenders

Listed below are the major types of lenders in Australia. There are a few others, but they offer such unusual loans you are not likely to ever need them. Generally, you should look to get a loan from one of these lenders.

Major Banks

The major banks, sometimes referred to as the Big Four, offer a complete banking service. This includes a branch network and telephone/Internet banking services. They generally offer automatic teller machine (ATM) cards and credit cards (Visa, MasterCard, and in some cases American Express) under their own brand names. Additional product features include chequebooks and deposit books (including the ability to cash cheques or make deposits at branches), along with a full range of deposit, investment, and insurance products.

👍PROS

- Large branch networks and overseas networks
- Call centres
- Insurance and investment products available
- Access to business finance
- Market-leading rates usually offered by subsidiaries

👎CONS

- Impersonal
- Usually don't offer market-leading rates or fees
- Average turnaround times

Example organisations:
ANZ Bank
Commonwealth Bank of Australia (CBA)
National Australia Bank (NAB)
Westpac

Brands owned by the major banks:
Bank of Melbourne (part of Westpac)
Bank SA (part of Westpac)

Bank West (part of CBA)
RAMS (part of Westpac)
St George Bank (part of Westpac)
UBank (part of NAB)

Regional Banks/Overseas Banks

Regional banks and overseas banks offer much the same service as the major banks, but usually with a smaller branch network. Often these banks operate using franchise models, either as community banks or as private operations. The branch networks can be a mixture of actual branches or lending-only storefronts.

☝PROS

- Branch networks (though smaller than the major banks)
- Call centres
- Insurance and investment products available
- Branches support the local community

☝CONS

- Smaller product range
- Usually don't offer market-leading rates or fees
- Average turnaround times

Example organisations:
Adelaide and Bendigo Bank
Arab Bank
Bank of Queensland
CitiBank
HSBC Bank
SunCorp

Branchless Banks

Branchless banks are simply banks without a branch network, or they may have a very limited network of a few branches. They offer the same services as the major banks, except they do not offer cash withdrawals or deposits from a branch network. These banks generally have never had a branch network and instead use a major bank as a deposit-taking branch (for example, if you are an ING customer, you can make a deposit at Westpac, but you can't get a balance or withdraw cash).

✑PROS

- Better rates and fees
- Call centres
- Usually offer all major products
- Generally specialize (e.g., direct sales teams or mortgage brokers)
- May support union or superfund members

✑CONS

- Nonexistent or very small branch network
- Smaller product range
- Harder to deal with; may require you to go through a mortgage broker

Example organisations:
AMP Bank
ING Bank
ME Bank

Non-Bank Lenders

Non-bank lenders can range from a single office up to hundreds of satellite or franchised offices, but they have some limitations. They may offer an ATM card or credit card that has been re-branded for them by a bank. They will often have telephone/Internet banking, but they may not have access to BPAY.

Non-bank lenders may also offer additional product features, including chequebooks and deposit books. As with branchless banks, you may not be able to cash cheques or make deposits over the counter. They often have other product alliances, such as Diners Club and American Express cards.

✋PROS

- Unusual products on offer
- Call centres
- Fast turnaround times
- Often offer market-leading rates
- Use mortgage brokers extensively
- Personal service

👎CONS

- No branch network
- Not all products are available
- Limited access to insurance or investment products

Example organisations:
Resimac
Aussie Home Loans

Building Societies

While their numbers have been reduced from over eight hundred in the 1950s to a handful today, building societies remain an alternative to traditional banks. Once called the "workingman's bank," today they offer a mix of balance-sheet and securitised lending. Most offer full-service banking with branches and all the products and features you would expect.

PROS

- Small branch networks
- Call centres
- Personal service
- Often not-for-profit

CONS

- Not all products are available
- Usually don't offer market-leading rates or fees
- Average turnaround times
- Limited access to insurance or investment products

Example organisations:
Newcastle Permanent Building Society
IMB

Credit Unions

Credit unions are much like the building societies. They have developed links with other credit unions to offer an effective network of branches and ATMs.

They will have most, if not all, of the products and features offered by banks.

PROS

- Small branch networks
- Call centres

- Personal service
- Often not-for-profit

☞CONS

- Not all products are available
- Usually don't offer market-leading rates or fees
- Average turnaround times
- Limited access to insurance or investment products

Example organisations:
Australian National Credit Union
Police and Nurses Credit Union

Mortgage Managers

Mortgage managers are resellers and managers of other lenders' products under their own brands. They carry out two major functions for the wholesaler (usually a non-bank lender), who is called the "funder."

They originate mortgage loans in accordance with the funder's credit policy and procedures.

They also manage the relationship with the borrower and carry out many of the administrative functions associated with the normal conduct of the loans.

The mortgage manager makes a profit by being paid a fee for managing the origination and day-to-day management of the borrowers on behalf of the lender.

Mortgage managers often have their own credit managers and can have faster approval turnaround times than bigger financial institutions.

They normally offer the full range of products offered by their funders.

🖒PROS

- Unusual products on offer
- Call centres
- Fast turnaround times
- Often offer market-leading rates
- Use mortgage brokers extensively
- Personal service

🖓CONS

- No branch network
- Not all products are available
- Limited access to Insurance or Investment products

Example organisations:
Home Loans Limited
Iden

Franchise Brokerages

In the mid-1990s, the concept of independent mortgage brokers forming franchises really took hold. These franchises have established themselves as real alternatives to major banks. They generally offer a wide range of products from a number of different lenders. They are usually keen to participate in their local communities and build businesses based on meeting the needs of their clients.

🖒PROS

- Call centres
- Fast turnaround times
- Offer a wide range of products from a number of lenders
- Personal service

☜CONS

+ Branch network is not used after you settle your loan
+ Not all products are available
+ Limited access to insurance or investment products

Example organisations:
Aussie
Mortgage Choice
Mortgage House of Australia

Non-Conforming Lenders

Non-conforming lenders have become a major part of the mortgage industry in Australia. These lenders specialise in providing finance to borrowers that do not qualify for a loan from traditional lending sources—borrowers who have missed payments or declared bankruptcy. These borrowers would have great difficulty in getting financing from a bank. There is a cost to the borrower, with interest rates higher than the major bank interest rates. But at least they are able to offer loans to borrowers who may not otherwise be able to get financing. However, in recent times they have found it difficult to provide new loans. This is mainly due to the international wholesale money markets being fearful of non-conforming loans since the Global Financial Crisis (GFC).

☝PROS

+ Loans designed for borrowers who can't get financing from major lenders due to credit history
+ Call centres
+ Fast turnaround times
+ Use mortgage brokers extensively
+ Personal service

☞ CONS

- No branch network
- Limited product range
- High interest rates and fees
- Limited or no access to insurance or investment products

Example organisations:
Bluestone Mortgages
Liberty Financial

Over the years, I have had loans from the major banks, branchless banks, and mortgage managers. I've never been a branch person—the queues always get to me! I've found calling the lenders is the best communication method, with e-mail next. Recently the big banks have made some real efforts to improve customer service, and they are putting pressure on the smaller banks and non-banks to provide top service.

Are you Rate-Sensitive?

As a borrower, you are considered rate-sensitive if you will become financially stressed should the interest rate of your loan increase. In general terms, the range for an increase that would result in stress is 1–2 percent. Borrowers on a low income or a fixed income often need a known, consistent repayment amount so they can budget for it.

If you are rate-sensitive, you should consider a fixed interest rate. These types of loans guarantee the rate will not change during the fixed term. However, fixed rates can be a double-edged sword, as you may fix at a rate which, due to later market conditions, is higher than the current variable rate. There is always the option of splitting your loan so that part is fixed and part is at a variable rate. This provides flexibility and allows additional repayments of principal.

Should You Fix?

A common question people looking for a new loan ask is, "Should I fix my interest rate?" The answer is not simple. First, you need to understand that fixed rate loans have exit fees, which can be very costly if you repay the loan before the end of the fixed rate period. You should first consider:

Are you rate-sensitive? If you really need a fixed rate, that may be a good idea, but only if you answer no to the next two questions.

1. Will you move in one to three years?

If you think you may have to move in the short term, you should look carefully at the exit costs of the loan. You should consider a variable interest rate loan with no break fees.

2. Will you be able to make any additional repayments? If you think you will be able to make extra or lump-sum repayments, it's a good idea to avoid fixed interest rate loans, which may charge you penalty fees or break rate fees if you pay more than the agreed-on repayments.

Let's look more closely at why fixed rate loans can be a double-edged sword for borrowers.

When it's good, it's good.

If you chose the right time to fix, you can win. For example, if you fixed for three years in July of 2004, you would have had a rate of 6.95 percent[2] when the standard variable rate was 7.05 percent. In the following three years, the standard variable rate increased, peaking at 7.45 percent. Your three-year fixed rate would have always been less than the variable rate!

When it's bad, it's bad.

If you chose the wrong time to fix, you lose. For example, if you fixed for three years in July 2008, you would have had a rate of 9.4 percent when the standard variable rate was 9.6 percent. In the following months, the reserve bank reduced interest rates to thirty-year lows. In April 2009, the standard variable rate had dropped to just 5.75 percent! At no time during the three-year fixed period would your loan

---

2 All interest rates cited in this section are provided by the Reserve Bank of Australia.

have been at a rate lower than the standard variable rate, and for long periods you would be paying more than 3 percent above the standard variable rate.

Some economists believe that the "normal" variable rate is in the 7–8 percent range. Therefore, any fixed rate less than this should, over time, be lower than the variable rate. However, this is based on averages over the last twenty years. In the last five years, we have seen the variable rate swing from a high of 9.6 percent to a low of 5.75 percent. We have entered a period of global financial uncertainty. I believe it is even harder now to predict interest rate changes and when to fix your loan.

It's simple. You can't see into the future to know if you will be better off. A lot of people have fixed at the wrong time and paid for it. So don't enter into a fixed rate expecting to win every time. Sometimes you will win; sometimes you will lose. Enter into a fixed rate if you'll be happy to pay the interest rate for the whole fixed period, regardless of what happens to the standard variable rate.

♠ **WARNING:** Some lenders offer fixed rate loans for periods up to ten or fifteen years. Generally, the longer the fixed rate term, the more likely you will be paying more than the variable rate. I would *never* fix for a period greater than five years.

I have only fixed once. I got what I thought was a good rate fixed for three years. For the first year I was well ahead, then the variable rate turned downward, and by the start of the second year I was paying well above the variable rate. In the end I think I came out about even, but I lost the opportunity to pay down my loan when the rates were low. As a result, I have never again fixed the full loan balance. I would consider fixing part of the balance for short periods of, say, three or less years.

So what do most people choose? While exact statistics are not available, it's generally believed the residential loan market is broken into the following product and interest rate categories:

- Variable interest rate loans (principal and interest repayments): 80 percent

- Variable interest rate loans (interest-only repayments including line of credit): 14 percent
- Fixed interest rate loans (both principal and interest and interest only): 6 percent

Basic or Full-Featured Loan: Which Should You Go With?

Will you need a flexible loan? Will you make lump-sum repayments and then need to redraw the money? If yes, avoid the basic products with limited features, as an upgrade will usually entail expensive fees. Fully featured loans offer the option to split some or all into fixed rate or line-of-credit products. I've never been a fan of basic loans, even when the rate is less than full-featured loans. I have found you need to keep your options open, and a basic loan removes options and charges fees and costs to add them back.

If you choose a full-featured loan and find you don't need the features, some lenders will allow you to downgrade to a basic loan—again, for a fee!

💣 **WARNING:** The information I have provided in this chapter is of a general nature, and I strongly recommend readers seek independent legal and financial advice prior to entering into any financial arrangement.

Chapter 3:

Loan types

● ●

In this Chapter:

➤ Loan types
➤ Pros and cons of loan types

● ●

Loan Types

The Australian home loan market is one of the most complex in the world. There are well over 2,500 different financial product offerings from several hundred lenders, and thousands of mortgage brokers. While the majority of these products are simple principal and interest loans branded for each lender, there are at least eighteen distinctly different product types.

These different products have been developed to meet the needs of many different types of consumers, and niche marketing has given the Australian consumer a vast array of products to choose from. It can be very easy to get confused when a large number of home loan products offer such a variety of different product features designed to meet the needs of different consumers.

While I have attempted to cover all the major home and investment loan products, the rate at which these products are developed is so fast, more and possibly different products will have been developed by the time this book is published.

Principal & Interest (P&I) Term Loans

This is the most common type of loan on the Australian market today. The P&I loan requires repayments made up of both principal and interest, so that the loan will "amortise," meaning the loan limit and balance gradually reduce over time until the loan is fully repaid. Usually a repayment will be required at least every month, often even if there have been some payments made in advance.

This type of loan is often perceived as being a reliable method of repaying your debt, as each repayment includes an amount of principal. Initially the amount is very small, and most of the repayment is interest. But over time this slowly changes, and by the end of the loan term the repayments become mostly principal.

Common features:

- Additional repayments allowed: you can make extra payments at any time.
- Redraw: repayments made in advance can be drawn back out.
- Redraw methods: direct credit, debit card, cheque, BPAY, Pay Anyone.
- Common payment frequencies: weekly, fortnightly, or monthly for regular repayments. One-off repayments are usually allowed for lump sums.
- Common payment methods: direct debit, salary credit, and BPAY.
- Internet and telephone banking access.
- Statements: usually at least 6 monthly, usually as at 31 December and 30 June.

Subcategories:
Basic Home Loans: P&I loans with reduced product features. These loans generally have a lower interest rate in exchange for fewer or limited product features. These products usually don't allow all

repayment frequencies, have minimum redraw amounts, and have minimum additional repayment amounts and transaction fees.They are often not portable, meaning if you sell your home you will have to repay the loan, even if you have a new security property and are willing to stay with the existing lender.

Fixed Interest Rate: P&I loans that have a fixed interest rate period. Fixed rates are not common, as they are a double-edged sword in that the interest rate will either be below or above the variable rate. If you are rate-sensitive, meaning you don't want to risk the variable rate increasing, fixed rates can be good. You know the exact repayment amount for the fixed period. Common fixed periods are one through five years. Seven, ten and fifteen year periods are also available.

Honeymoon: P&I Loans in which there is a discounted introductory interest rate. Honeymoon, or introductory rate loans, offer you the opportunity to have a lower interest rate for a short period, usually from six months to two years. It is important to note that the honeymoon rate usually converts to a premium variable rate higher than the lender's standard variable rate. The initial entry fees can also sometimes be higher.

Principal and interest repayment graph:

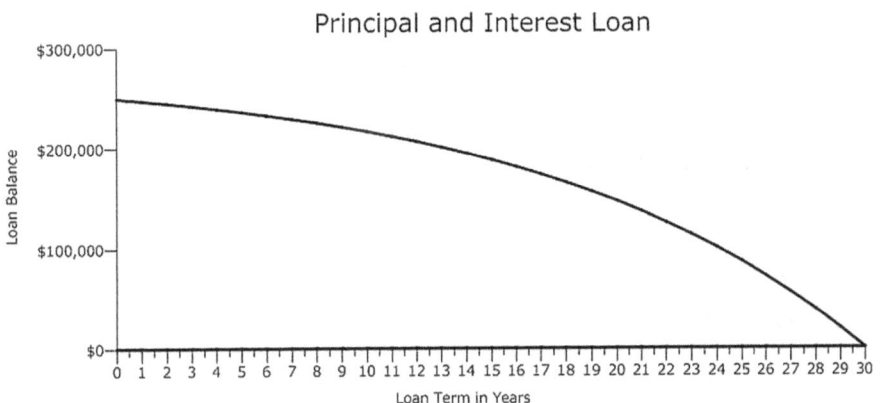

Interest Only (IO) Term Loans

This is an increasingly common feature available for new loans. For a period at the beginning of a loan, only interest is paid. The principal remains the same during the interest only period. The loan converts to principal and interest at the end of the interest only period, and the balance gradually reduces over the remaining term of the loan. Once they do commence, the principal and interest repayments will of course be higher than a normal P&I loan because the term remaining to repay has been decreased by the interest only period. These loans are used mainly for investments, as the repayment amount is reduced to the minimum, aiding cash flow and maximising tax deductibility.

Common features:

- Interest only periods of one through five years or ten years.
- Additional repayments: you can make extra payments at any time.
- Redraw: repayments made in advance can be drawn back out.
- Redraw methods: direct credit, debit card, cheque, BPAY, Pay Anyone.
- Common payment frequencies: weekly, fortnightly, or monthly for regular repayments. One-off repayments are usually allowed for lump sums. It is common for interest only loans to have a monthly payment requirement.
- Common payment methods: direct debit, salary credit, and BPAY.
- Internet and telephone banking access.
- Statements: usually monthly but at least 6 monthly, usually as at 31 December and 30 June.

Subcategories:
Basic Home Loan: see P&I loans above.
Fixed Interest Rate: see P&I loans above.
Honeymoon: see P&I loans above.

Interest only converting to principal and interest repayment graph:

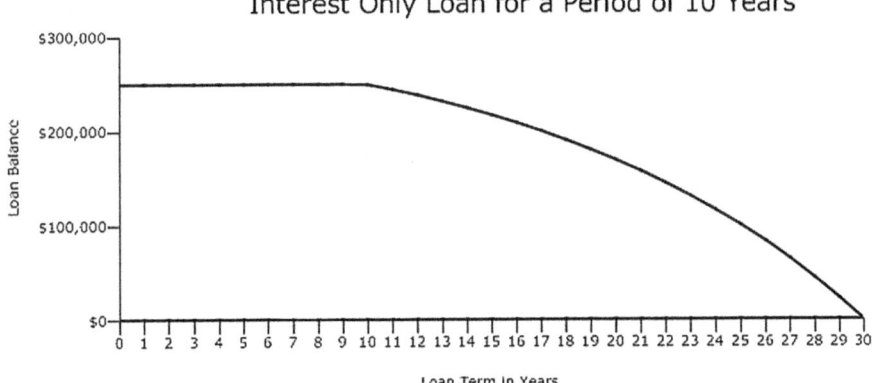

Interest Only Loan for a Period of 10 Years

Line of Credit

Lines of credit are increasingly common in the home loan market. The line of credit is a revolving credit product. The loan has a set limit and interest only repayments. You may redraw and repay as much principal as you wish. Lines of credit are very much like an overdraft in that you can use any available funds within the limit.

These loans often have the most features and can include access methods such as credit cards, ATM cards, and chequebooks. Additional payments can be made by direct salary crediting, direct debit, or over-the-counter deposits at bank branches with deposit books. Usually the minimum repayment will be the amount of interest charged in the current month.

Common features:

- Revolving credit period of ten, fifteen, twenty, twenty-five, or thirty years.

- Additional repayments: you can make extra payments at any time.

- Redraw: the loan can be drawn up to its limit at any time.

- Redraw methods: direct credit, debit card, cheque, BPAY, Pay Anyone.

- Common payment frequencies: monthly for normal payments. One-off for lump sums.

- Common payment methods: direct debit, salary credit, BPAY, and over the counter by deposit book.

- Internet and telephone banking access.

- Statements: monthly.

Subcategories:

Capitalising Line of Credit: A capitalising line of credit allows you to stop making payments of interest so long as the loan has not reached its limit. For example, you may have a limit of $100,000 drawn to $50,000. During the month, $500 of interest accrues and is added to the loan, taking the balance to $50,500. You do not need to make a repayment, as the loan is within its $100,000 limit.

Evergreen Line of Credit or No-Term Line of Credit: A line of credit that does not have a final repayment date. In effect, the loan can continue for as long as you can repay it. Usually subject to an annual review at the lender's discretion.

Honeymoon or Introductory Line of Credit: A line of credit with an introductory interest rate lower than the standard rate, usually for a term of six or twelve months.

Amortising Line of Credit: A line of credit that has a reducing or amortising limit. This product falls halfway between a principal and interest loan and a line of credit. It offers all the benefits of a line of credit: being able to redraw and repay within the limit, capitalisation, and flexible access methods. It also has the safety net of a principal and interest loan in that the limit will reduce to nil by the end of the set term, usually thirty years. Not a common product offering, but it does have some key advantages over the standard line of credit for people who may fear never repaying their loans.

Line of credit repayment graph:

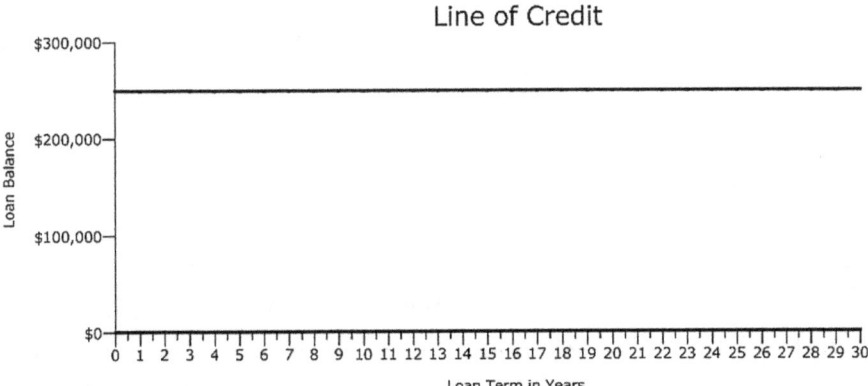

Construction Loans

Construction loans allow you to borrow the cost of building a home, often including the cost of the purchase of the land (sometimes called a house and land package loan). Generally, construction loans are interest only during the construction period and then convert to a standard principal and interest loan.

Common features:

- Interest only during the construction period (usually a maximum of twelve months).

- Additional repayments: usually not allowed during construction, but available after construction is completed.

- Redraw: not usually allowed during the construction period, but available after construction is completed.

- Common payment frequencies: monthly interest only during construction, then weekly, fortnightly, or monthly for regular repayments. One-off repayments usually discouraged during the construction period.

- Common payment methods: direct debit, salary credit, and BPAY.

- Internet and telephone banking access.
- Statements: usually monthly during construction; but often 6 monthly as at 31 December and 30 June.

Subcategories:

Owner Builder: A construction loan in which you are the builder. These loans are generally seen as more risky by lenders. Owner builders are often inexperienced and routinely underestimate the total cost to complete construction. As a result, the maximum loan and loan to value ratio (LVR) amounts are generally lower. This means you can usually only borrow up to 60–70 percent of the value of the completed property.

Annual Fee or Pro Pack Loans

Lenders often call these loans "Pro Packs." However, they are better described as annual-fee loans, as the objective of the product is to attract large loans, not just loans to professionals such as solicitors or accountants. These days, virtually every Australian home loan lender has a loan that attracts borrowers with an annual fee as a trade-off for a reduced interest rate, the discounts offer vary from 0.25 – 0.90 percent. In the past, the banks would have had you believe that such loans were only available to high-income professionals with larger home and investment loans, but today virtually anyone requiring a loan of $250,000 or more can access such a home-loan product.

But with these fees ranging from $200 up to a whopping $500 per year, are these loans really offering value for the money? What is clear is that, as the amount of these loans increases, the trade-off between a lower interest rate and the annual fee amount becomes more attractive. But to really determine if such a product will benefit you and your financial position, you need to consider three things:

1. Size does matter. Simply put, the bigger the loan, the bigger the relative saving in interest. If you receive an interest rate discount of 0.25 percent on a $250,000 loan, your maximum saving will be $625 per annum. But if your loan was $600,000, the saving would be up to $1,500.

2. Paying the fee in arrears is better value. If a lender is asking for an annual fee in advance, they are having your cake and eating it too! After all, it will take you the full year to achieve the corresponding benefit in reduced interest.

3. Your financial plans affect the outcome, so plan well. If you receive a discount of 0.25 percent on a $250,000 loan and make the minimum repayments over the full term of the loan (usually thirty years), you will save a maximum of $14,699 (so long as you pay the annual fee in full and don't add it to the balance of your loan). However, if you were to repay an extra $50 per month, you would save well over $32,000!

Depending on the individual situation, an annual-fee loan may or may not be good value. Certainly for anyone with a loan of less than $250,000, the cost of the annual fee is debatable. Remember, even if you save $625, you may be paying an annual fee of $500, giving you a net saving of just $125 per year.

Common features:

- See principal and interest loans.

Basic Home Loans

The basic home loan is a simplified product, usually based on a standard principal and interest or interest-only loan. The lender offers the product at a reduced interest rate and, to compensate for the loss of interest revenue, reduces the features available or charges higher transaction fees. The lender is not expecting to have to offer a lot of service for these loans, as they are targeted at borrowers seeking a simple lending solution.

Often the transactions available are limited, or fees apply.

WARNING: Beware of these loans because the minute you do need some service or flexibility, the lender will not hesitate to up-sell you to a fully featured product—for a hefty fee, of course!

Common features:

- See principal and interest loans.

Bridging Loans

So called because they bridge a gap for borrowers who have an existing home by providing a loan to purchase a new property while selling the first property. These loans exist because the settlement of the existing security property and the new property can't happen at the same time. For a short bridging period, you may have two loans: one for your existing home and another for your new home. Many lenders offer bridging loans at standard home-loan interest rates, sometimes even with the ability to capitalise interest until the existing property is sold. You do need to be very careful with the size of your debt and the cost of these kinds of loans, but they certainly provide the flexibility to buy a new property before selling your existing one.

Example: A couple has a home worth $500,000 with a mortgage of $200,000. They want to upgrade homes, but don't want the inconvenience of moving to a rental property and then to their new home. They are looking at a new property for $650,000 and have no savings. If they use bridging finance, they will have total borrowings of $200,000 (existing) + $650,000 (new purchase) + $35,000 (costs) = $885,000. They will have this loan for the time it takes them to settle the sale of their current property after purchasing the new one. Once they sell their existing home (for $500,000), their mortgage would then reduce to $485,000 plus bridging costs. During the bridging finance period, they continue to make their existing loan repayments. However, the interest on the $650,000 loan for the new property capitalises (adds to the loan). Mostly, bridging loans are for a maximum period of three months. The couple can therefore have a maximum loan (after the bridging period) of $502,000. If the couple has not sold their existing home at the end of the three month period, they will likely have to commence making at least interest repayments on the bridging loan.

First-Home Owner Loans

Some lenders offer loans targeted at the first-home owner market. These loans often have discounts on application fees and Lender's Mortgage Insurance (LMI) fees. Some lenders allow first home owners to access up to 100 percent of the property value. A few even lend up to 105 percent of the property value, effectively allowing the borrower to also fund the associated costs of purchasing their home. There can be disadvantages with these loans, though, including higher interest rates and expensive ongoing fees.

Common features:

• See principal and interest loans.

Subcategories:

Fixed Interest Rate: see principal and interest loans. The fixed rate periods may be limited.

Family Pledge Loan

The family pledge loan was developed to allow parents or other relatives of the borrowers to assist by providing additional security, this allows the borrowers to gain access to loans without the need to pay expensive LMI fees. The loan can be for 100 percent of the value of the property plus all costs. The family pledge loan works by having a parent or other family member guarantee part of the loan. The amount guaranteed is set at the outset of the loan. This provides peace of mind for the guarantors, who are only ever liable for a set amount. Usually the family member who offers the guarantee will also have a mortgage with the lender, so their property is also at risk if the borrowers default!

Common features:

• See principal and interest loans.

Subcategories:
Fixed interest rate options

Example: A couple wants to purchase their first home for $500,000. They have no deposit, and the costs are expected to be $50,000. So they are seeking a loan of $550,000. This means they are seeking a loan of 110 percent of the security property value, a 110 percent loan to value ratio (LVR) lend. If they were to seek a non-family pledge loan, the lender would not be able to provide a loan greater than 97 percent. Even a 97 percent LVR lend would require LMI, which would cost an additional $14,625. The lender instead takes a guarantee from one of the borrower's parents. This means the lender has two forms of security, the mortgaged house and a guarantee.

Low Doc Loans

Low Doc loans are designed mainly for people who have some equity (or a deposit) but who may have trouble showing evidence of their income levels, such as the self-employed or borrowers who have irregular incomes.

In the past, Low Doc loans had significantly higher interest rates than standard loans and therefore were generally only used as a last resort. Slowly the rates moved down to the point where a number of lenders offered these loans at standard interest rates. Then came the GFC of 2008–09, and the availability of Low Doc loans began to dry up as interest rates increased and financial institutions reassessed the credit risks and funding costs.

Most lenders will allow a loan of up to 80 percent of the value of the property you provide as security. Some lenders may even allow up to 90 percent or 95 percent, although interest rates are often higher in these situations. Mortgage insurance is often required, and is in most cases payable by the borrower.

The lender will still need to complete a credit assessment, but with Low Doc loans the lender has to assess the credit based on either:

• Your declaration of income and affordability, or

• A declaration of affordability only

In a declaration of income and affordability, the borrowers provide the lender with a declaration of how much they earn. They also state that they can afford the repayments. The lender will use the declared income amount to assess if the borrower is able to afford the repayments. This is done in the same manner as a loan where full details of income, including evidence, are provided.

Lenders and/or mortgage brokers are still required to take reasonable steps to verify the financial position of the borrower. This is at odds with the concept of a Low Doc loan, where the borrower does not need to provide evidence of income. To get around this problem, lenders have come up with loan products that can best be described as "alternative verification."

By providing some documents as evidence of income, lenders can fulfil their obligations under the National Consumer Credit Protection Act (NCCP) without requiring your tax returns. The most common documents that lenders ask for are:

- **BAS statements.** A lender may ask for twelve months of Business Activity Statements to verify your turnover and from that estimate your income.

- **Trading statements.** A lender may ask for six months of bank account statements for your business to verify your turnover and from that estimate your income.

- **Accountant's letter.** A lender may have a specific accountant's letter template for your accountant to sign to confirm your income.

In a declaration of affordability only, the borrowers do not provide the lender with any details of their income; the borrowers simply declare they are able to afford the repayments. These loans are sometimes called No Doc loans, as there is no requirement for actual documents evidencing income. This is generally much riskier for the lenders, as they cannot even complete a basic estimate of the borrower's ability to repay. Generally this type of Low Doc loan will have a limited LVR, usually less than 70 percent. The NCCP introduced strong requirements for lenders to prove borrowers can afford to repay loans without falling into financial hardship. No Doc loans may disappear as a result of this requirement, or they may be available only to company or trust borrowers.

Common features:

- See principal and interest loans.

Subcategories:
Fixed interest rate options

Example: John might have $250,000 on deposit and may want to purchase a $1 million property, but he may not be able to prove he earns enough money to afford the loan. Being self-employed, John might have always earned a good income in the past but may have been slow in getting tax returns done. Or he may receive income in lump sums rather than consistently over the course of each year. The lender may be able to offer John a loan of $800,000, 80 percent of the property value. John will need to provide a declaration of income and affordability, and he will need to pass the lender's other credit assessments and requirements, such as having an Australian Business Number (ABN) and a clear credit history.

Non-Conforming Loans

Non-conforming loans are designed mainly for people who have some equity (or a deposit) but who may have trouble getting a loan from a traditional lender. They may have been in arrears, had defaults, or been made bankrupt.

Non-conforming loans can have significantly higher interest rates than standard loans. The recent credit crunch has seen non-conforming loan interest rates increase even further as financial institutions reassess the credit risks and funding costs.

The cost of funding these loans has increased to a point where most lenders have stopped offering them. It is becoming very difficult to find non-conforming loans in the current market. Even if they return, it is likely the credit policies will be very restricted, and few applications are likely to be approved.

Common features:

- Restrictive loan amounts, often less than 80 percent of the value of the security property.

- High interest rates.

- High application fees.

- Interest-only period of one through five years or ten years.

- Additional repayments can be made at any time.

- Redraw: repayments made in advance can be drawn back out.

- Redraw methods: direct credit, debit card, Pay Anyone.

- Common payment frequencies: weekly, fortnightly, or monthly for regular repayments. One-off repayments are usually allowed for lump sums.

- Common payment methods: direct debit, salary credit.

- Internet and telephone banking access.

- Statements: usually at least 6 monthly, usually as at 31 December and 30 June.

Subcategories:
Fixed interest rate options

Example: Geoff has a home loan of $250,000 that is currently in arrears. He also has a number of defaults in his credit file (mainly for credit cards and mobile phone contracts). He has been unemployed but now has a job. Generally, most lenders will not allow Geoff to refinance as he is in arrears, has defaults, and is in a new job. The nonconforming lender may well refinance Geoff's loan; however, it will be at a higher interest rate.

Interest In Advance Loans

Some lenders allow you to pay the interest on their loans in advance. This can be beneficial when the loan is for investment purposes. It is a slightly complex loan, as only interest paid in the current financial year can be a tax deduction in the current tax year. These types of transactions are used by investors to effectively manipulate their income for tax purposes, by moving an expense, the interest into the current tax year. As interest is paid in advance, the loan must be interest only and for a fixed interest rate.

Common features:

- Interest-only period of one year (rolling each year).

- The interest rate will be fixed for at least one year.

- Additional repayments are not allowed, or if allowed do not reduce the interest cost.

- Redraw generally not allowed.

- Interest is paid in advance in a single lump sum.

- Internet and telephone banking access for review only.

- Statements are usually at least 6 monthly, usually as at 31 December and 30 June.

🖐**TIP:** As with anything you pay for in advance, ask for and expect a discount! You should get a lower rate for paying all your interest up to a year in advance.

Reverse Mortgages

Reverse mortgages allow borrowers, usually retired people who own their homes and are mortgage-free, to borrow cash against the value of their home as a lump sum, a regular stream of income, or a combination of both. With this type of loan, you don't have to make regular repayments. The loan balance just keeps increasing, with interest being added until the owner leaves the property and moves into care, sells the home, or dies. When the loan ends, the owner or the owner's estate must repay the balance, usually out of the proceeds of the sale of the property.

Each year the fees and interest the borrower would ordinarily pay are added to the loan balance. Over time, interest is charged on the interest, and that builds up the total amount owed.

There is a risk that the amount of the loan may increase to a point where it is more than the value of the property. This is called negative equity. Some, but not all, reverse mortgage products guarantee that if this happens, you will not have to repay more than the value of the property (a no negative equity guarantee). But owners may lose this protection if they don't meet the terms and conditions of the loan—for example, if the property is not maintained in a good state of repair.

The maximum loan amount is usually limited to between 15 percent and 40 percent of the value of the property, depending on the age of the owner at the time of application. Generally, the older the owners, the more they can borrow. In the case of a couple who are both owners of the property, the amount borrowed is based on the age of the youngest borrower.

Generally, the interest rate is fixed for the term of the loan; however, some products are at a variable rate. The actual interest rate will usually be higher than a standard loan; however, you do not need to have an income to qualify for the loan.

It's important to seek independent financial advice before entering in to a reverse mortgage.

⏍ **TIP:** Any form of compounding interest can quickly raise the debt levels close to the value of the security property. Also, the loan may affect eligibility for a pension.

Example: Jim is sixty-five years old and retired. He owns his home and is mortgage-free. Jim's home is valued at $500,000, and he has opted to have a reverse mortgage of 15 percent of the value of the home, or $75,000. The reverse mortgage is at a fixed rate of 11 percent. Over the next fifteen years, the property will increase in value at a rate of 4 percent per year. If Jim moves out of his home to a rest home in fifteen years, the reverse mortgage balance will be $358,000, while the property value will have increased to $900,000. So Jim will have had the benefit of the $75,000 lump sum for fifteen years and still own more than $500,000 of his property when he leaves the house.

Equity Finance Mortgage (EFM)

An EFM generally operates with a traditional home loan. Together they let you delay some of the expense of a traditional home loan to later on, when you eventually sell the property. The equity finance portion, which is generally up to 20 percent of the value of a property, is funded by an equity finance mortgage and secured by a second mortgage, on which you pay 0 percent interest. The EFM lender trades off the loss of interest income by taking up to 40 percent of any future capital gains or 20 percent of any capital losses on the property.

This product allows you to purchase a more valuable home, take on lower loan repayments, and may also avoid or reduce LMI, as the loan from the traditional lender may be below the LVR limit of 80 percent.

When the property is sold or the EFM loan is repaid for any other reason, you repay the EFM amount originally borrowed plus up to a 40 percent share of any increase in the value of the property.

This product can also allow someone who would otherwise be unable to save up a deposit the opportunity to purchase a property.

Example: Joan is saving for her first home and has current savings of $10,000. She wishes to purchase a townhouse for $450,000. If she were to use her savings of $10,000, she would have a loan of $440,000 or a 98 percent LVR. This would mean she would not qualify for a standard loan. An EFM offers Joan the ability to purchase the property without the need for LMI and also reduce her repayments by borrowing less. Joan takes an EFM of 20 percent, or $90,000, meaning she needs a standard loan of $360,000, resulting in an LVR of 80 percent. Joan then does not require LMI and will be making repayments on a loan $90,000 less than the traditional loan.

Five years later, Joan sells the townhouse for $750,000. She repays the EFM lender's original investment of $90,000 plus $120,000 (being 40 percent of the $300,000 capital gain). As you can see, the EFM lender has made a handsome profit. However, the EFM lender may have to wait up to thirty years for any return. And Joan would not have been able to purchase the property without the additional EFM funds.

Reduced Repayment Loans

This type of loan allows for part of the interest charge each month to be capitalised to the loan account. This means that during the reduced repayment term, the loan actually grows in size. These loans are often targeted at investors looking to increase their cash flow for a period. In a rising property market, the concept of reduced repayment for an amount of capitalisation seems reasonable. But when property prices are falling or rising at a much lower rate, there is a risk of the property being worth less than the loan amount at the end of the reduced repayment term.

These loans will mostly be on a variable rate and therefore subject to normal rate increases. Any rate rise would further increase the capitalisation, making the repayments after the reduced repayment term even greater.

♠* **WARNING:** It is very important to seek independent financial advice regarding reduced repayment loans, as any form of capitalising interest can quickly raise the debt levels close to the value of the security property.

HECS Debt Home Loans

A HECS loan allows recent graduates to repay their HECS debt and purchase a home at the same time. Generally this type of loan is at a higher interest rate and has strict credit requirements, including employment in specific fields, such as the legal industry. The maximum loan amount, however, is often as much as 130 percent of the property value.

The loan may offer a graduate with no deposit entry into the housing market, but costly fees make this type of loan a rarity in today's market.

Self-Managed Super Fund Loans

Recent changes to Australian superannuation legislation now allow self-managed super funds to invest directly in real estate and get mortgage loans in the name of the super trust. The tax benefits are based on making loan repayments from before-tax dollars rather than after-tax dollars.

The loan structure is complex and generally requires at least one trust and guarantees from the beneficiaries of the trust. This can result in higher legal costs and complex management issues. Currently only a limited number of non-bank lenders are offering self-managed super fund loans, generally at higher interest rates.

Tracker Loans

Tracker loans are variable rate loans (either principal and interest or interest only) that track their actual rates based on a predefined requirement. Usually the loan will track its rate based on a published government interest rate or the average of the big banks. Tracker rates are generally applicable for the first two years, after which time the loan converts to the lender's standard variable interest rate.

Example: ABC Bank, a small regional bank, offers a tracker loan 0.50 percent lower than the average of the big four banks. So if the average of the big four banks is 9.65 percent, the tracker loan will be set at 9.15 percent. The loan is still variable, so any increase or decrease in the average rate offered by the big four banks will result in a change to the tracker loan.

Other Loan Options
Offset Accounts

An offset account is not a loan in real terms; it is an option offered by some lenders that allows you to deposit funds to a savings account. Instead of earning interest, the balance of the savings account is deducted from the loan, and less interest accrues on the loan as a result. This is where the term offset comes from. The savings account balance is offset against the loan. Offset accounts are usually only offered by deposit-taking institutions such as banks. The accounts are often accessible by the banking system, so they can also be used for paying bills over the Internet or by BPAY. They may also have ATM card access.

A similar result can be achieved in loans where extra repayments are allowed. Off Set has some tax benefits as the interest saved is not taxable therefore the saving is at the actual rate of the loan.

I currently have an off set account and have saved hundreds of dollars by parking extra money in the account, even if it's for a few days.

Extended Term Loans

Over time the maximum available loan term in Australia has become longer and longer, with some lenders now offering loan terms of thirty-five and forty years. While these longer terms were introduced in an effort to assist with affordability, the reality is that the average monthly repayment is reduced by a very small amount when compared to the more usual thirty-year loan term.

Example: The monthly repayments for a loan of $250,000 over thirty years at an interest rate of 9.32 percent are $2,069.38. The same loan repayments for a loan with a term of thirty-five years are $2,020.04, a reduction of just $49.34 per month. However, if you were to simply make interest only repayments for the first five years, the monthly repayment would be $1,941.66, a reduction of more than $100 per month. So I would not recommend these loans. If you are looking for the smallest possible monthly repayment, interest only is the better option.

Global Limit Loans

A global limit loan will have a number of sub-accounts, or splits. Each split will have as its loan limit set to the limit of the total loan. This means that it is possible to fully draw the loan to any single account. This allows for purpose-specific redraw. For example, the first split account may be for personal use, while the second is used for investment purposes. Redraw that builds up in the personal split account can later be drawn from the investment account and used for further investment purposes, making the interest payable on the redraw tax-deductible.

Mortgage Minimisation

The term mortgage minimisation was coined in the early 90s as borrowers found loan products that allowed them to put all their income directly into the loan account. By depositing all income directly into the loan, the balance was reduced and, as a result, the amount of interest charged was also reduced. A credit card would be used for all day-to-day spending. In turn, the credit card was then paid from the loan prior to any interest being chargeable on it. In this manner the borrower would reduce the amount of interest paid on the loan and repay the debt faster. The credit card was cleared monthly in full, therefore accruing no interest.

This way of managing finances was used as a selling tool by mortgage brokers. However, a high number of borrowers ended up increasing their debt, as they simply could not budget successfully.

High LVR Loans

The lending industry has offered high LVR loans, where you borrow more than 94 percent of the security property value for a long time. However, these types of loans are inherently more risky for the lender. The main providers of high LVR loans have in the past been the non-bank lenders, who insure the risk with LMI. However, many of these lenders have either removed the high LVR products or placed extreme limitations on them. While some high LVR loans still exist, they are generally so expensive to establish that you are better off saving a bigger deposit.

The risk you take as a borrower by having little, zero, or negative equity in your property is that any reduction in the value of your property could be extremely damaging financially. If you have negative equity, you will be in a position of not being able to sell the property without taking a loss. This of course means you are stuck in the property until the value increases with the general property market or you pay down your debt.

The Pros and Cons of Loan Types

When you are considering different loan types, it's important that you compare products based on their individual strengths and weaknesses.

While each loan product offered in the market will be different, the differences are usually in fees, charges, and available product features. Fundamentally there are only three product types: variable rate loans (principal and interest or interest-only repayment), fixed rate loans (also principal and interest or interest-only repayment), and lines of credit.

Variable Rate Principal and Interest

☝PROS

* Interest rate is not fixed and may reduce if market conditions change
* Interest rates are generally lower than fixed rates
* You are free to make additional repayments without penalty at any time
* Often very flexible, allowing for redraws, additional advances, and repayment holidays
* Repayments can be weekly, fortnightly, or monthly

☟CONS

* Interest rate is not fixed, and if market conditions change the interest rate may increase
* Interest rates may change at any time, so you do not have certainty of repayment amount

Variable Rate Interest Only

See all of the above for variable rate principal and interest plus:

☝PROS

* As you are only paying interest and not principal, the repayment will be lower than a principal and interest loan

- Interest only repayments are often used for investment proper-ties, as the actual cost of the investment is clear to the ATO

☞CONS

- As you are only paying interest the loan balance will not reduce during the interest only term
- Repayments are usually monthly only if you wish to pay the exact (minimum) amount of interest

Fixed Rate Loans (Both Principal and Interest and Interest Only)

☝PROS

- Interest rate is fixed. Terms include one through five years and ten years, longer in some cases
- Repayments are set during the fixed rate period, meaning you will know exactly how much you need to pay. If you are rate-sensitive, meaning you need to know how much you will pay for budgeting purposes, this can be a real benefit
- Repayments can be weekly, fortnightly, or monthly
- Limited ability to make lump-sum repayments without penalty (usually a small amount per year is penalty-free)

☞CONS

- Interest rate is fixed, so if market conditions move the variable interest rates down, you will continue to pay the fixed rate for the remaining fixed term
- If you repay the loan in part or in full (a break rate event) you may be charged a break rate fee. The fee could be very high depending on the interest rate you fixed and the term remaining

Lines of Credit

✦PROS

- Interest rate is not fixed and may reduce if market conditions change
- You are free to make additional repayments without penalty at any time
- You are free to redraw up to your limit at any time. This is useful for investors, as it means you can make purchases without the need to apply for additional lending

✦CONS

- Interest rate is not fixed; if market conditions change, the rate may increase
- Interest rate may change at any time, meaning you do not have certainty of the repayment amount
- Repayments are usually monthly only

Other product features to consider: Offset Accounts

✦PROS

- Any credit funds you have in your offset account reduce the balance of your loan account for the purposes of charging interest
- You still have full control over your credit funds in your offset account and are able to withdraw them at any time, avoiding redraw fees

Split Accounts

A loan split account allows you to separate your loan into a number of different product types, such as variable and fixed. This means you can fix part of your loan so you know how much you will pay on that split. You can leave part variable, allowing you to make extra repayments and benefit from any variable rate reductions while limiting the impact of variable rate increases. You may choose to add a line of credit, either to use as a day-to-day transaction account (in a similar manner to an offset account) or for investment purposes, such as purchasing shares.

✎ **TIP:** Always get independent financial advice from an accountant, mortgage broker, solicitor, or your bank. No one can predict what will happen to interest rates in the future, so you need to be happy with the interest rate and repayment type (principal and interest or interest only) you choose, as you will not be able to change them without some costs.

I have had interest only loans in the past. They were good when we first bought our home, as the repayments were lower. However, I now have a principal and interest loan with an offset account, and it works well for me, as I park extra funds in my offset account.

This gives me the best of both worlds. I have access to my extra funds, and at the same time the interest charge is reduced.

Chapter 4:

Fees

• •

In this Chapter:

➤ Up-front fees
➤ Ongoing fees
➤ Are fees legal?

• •

enders often offer a discounted interest rate to attract the borrower and then look to fee income to offset the cost of the discounted interest rate. As an outcome, the industry has in recent years been looking more and more to fees as an income source. The lending market has become very competitive, and interest rates are a key driver of sales. In such a competitive market, lenders are very aware they must compete on rate first. However, very few consumers take into account the cost of fees when evaluating the loans on offer.

You should take into account the ongoing cost of fees, as they can soon add up! Some lenders charge transaction fees, monthly account-keeping fees, or annual fees on their home loans.

*TIP:** Don't get trapped in a high-fee loan. Find out what you are likely to end up paying before you agree to take the loan! A monthly fee of just $12 will cost you $760 in just five years.

Up-Front Fees
Application/Valuation

Application fees are very common and generally cover the cost to the lender of processing the loan. Often these fees are paid on application, meaning when you complete the application form. The valuation fee covers the cost of the valuation of the security property. Generally these fees are not income sources for lenders, but beware: often application fees can be negotiated and sometimes even waived.

✋**TIP:** In today's competitive lending environment, you can and should ask for application fees to be waived. Lenders are eager to get your business, and most will happily waive or reduce application fees!

You will be in a stronger position to negotiate fees if you also intend to buy other services, such as transactional bank accounts or insurance.

Lender's Mortgage Insurance

LMI can easily add a few thousand dollars to the cost of a home loan. You should consider whether it's better to save for a bigger deposit and therefore reduce the cost of the LMI premium or eliminate the need for it. Also, the insurance covers the lender, not you, and it's also almost impossible to get a refund of LMI premiums.

Legal Fees

The cost of the lender's solicitor and settlement fees often form part of the initial fees. And then of course, don't forget your own conveyancer or solicitor, who will want to be paid as well!

Ongoing Fees

Common ongoing fees include annual fees, review fees, and management fees. These can be very significant, too, as shown in the following table.

Annual Fee Amount	5 Years	25 Years	30 Years
$199	$995	$4,975	$5,970
$249	$1,248	$6,225	$7,470
$399	$1,995	$9,975	$11,970

Activity-Based Fees

As well as known fees, it's important to understand that lenders will charge other fees depending on how you manage your loan. As such, it is difficult to calculate the true cost of all fees. Below is a list of some generic fees. These fees are not classed as transaction fees, as the lender does not expect to have to charge them in the normal life of a loan, assuming all repayments are made on time and no changes are requested by the borrower.

- Dishonour fees
- Arrears fees/over limit fees
- Consent fees
- Statement reissue fees

These fees can cost you from a few dollars to hundreds of dollars.

Transaction Fees

Transaction fees are fees the lender is expecting to charge during the life of the loan. These fees are levied as you use the loan facility. These fees can soon add up, and they range from a few cents to five dollars depending on the loan type. The table below assumes just five transactions per month.

Transaction Fee Amount	5 Years	25 Years	30 Years
$0.50	$150	$750	$900
$1	$300	$1,500	$1,800
$5	$1,500	$7,500	$9,000

Example: Mr. and Mrs. Green have a home loan that is their main working account. They make five transactions per month and have an interest rate of 7 percent. The loan is for $220,000 with a LVR of 90 percent. Listed below are the fees chargeable if the loan remains with the same lender for five years. This list includes the exit fees chargeable.

Fee Name	Details	Total Fee
Application	Paid on application	$550
Valuation Fee	Paid on application	$220
Lenders Mortgage Insurance (LMI)	Paid on settlement	$3,075
Lenders Panel Solicitor Professional Fees	Paid on settlement	$750
Settlement Fee (paid to Lender)	Paid on settlement	$25
Initial Annual Fee (paid to Lender)	Paid on settlement	$399
Mortgage Registration Fee (State Fee)	Paid on settlement	$90
Discharge of Mortgage Fee (State Fee)	Paid on settlement	$90
Total of Initial Fees and Charges		**$5,199**
Ongoing and Exit Fees		
Annual Fees	$399 each year	$1,995
Dishonour Fees	$50 twice	$100
Over Limit Fee	$100 once	$100
Withdrawal Fees	5 transactions per month at $1 each	$300
Discharge Fee (payable to the Lender at discharge of the mortgage)	Flat Fee	$500
Total Ongoing Fees		**$2,995**
Total Fee over 5 Years		**$8,194**

Some facts:

- In this conservative example, the total fees chargeable (including government fees and costs) exceed $8,000!
- The single biggest fee is the LMI premium
- The annual fee accounts for 24 percent of the total fees

You can save a reasonable amount of money by being aware of fees prior to taking out a loan.

Exit Fees

The federal government has recently banned loan exit fees. However, if you have a loan which settled prior to 1 July 2011, any exit fee will still apply.

Discharge Fees

A discharge fee is payable when you repay your loan, either at the end of its term or when you refinance. The lender charges this fee to cover costs involved with the production of the discharge of mortgage documents and attending the settlement. The fee is usually a flat fee ranging from $100 to $500.

Fixed Rate Break Fees

Fixed rate break fees are applied when you choose to end a fixed rate term before the end of the fixed period.

It's important to understand that these fees can be very expensive, so it's wise to go into fixed rates with your eyes open! A great rate today may be uncompetitive in as little as a few months.

The fee represents the actual loss the lender will make by no longer having the fixed rate loan. As the lender will have entered into an arrangement with another party to have the funds fixed for that term, the lender either has to pay out the loan or resell the fixed rate, possibly for a loss at the current rates for the remaining term.

Example: Mr. and Mrs. Smith decided to fix their home loan in early June 2008 for five years at 9.05 percent. The variable rates shortly thereafter reached 9.56 percent, and the Smiths were very pleased with their decision. However, just a few months later the variable rate began to go down, and by November 2008 it had dropped to 7.71 percent. The fixed rate for five years had dropped to 7.39 percent. The Smiths decided to break out of the 9.05 percent fixed rate just five months after taking it out. They faced a rate break fee of $38,958!

This example uses a generic approach to calculate the loss to the lender. Some lenders may calculate their fees differently or include administrative fees in addition to the break costs. Some lenders offer a limited discount either for a set dollar amount (i.e., no fee for the first $10,000 prepaid) or an amount calculated based on the number of months remaining.

It's important to enter into a fixed rate knowing that it may not be competitive for its entire term.

🖉 **TIP:** Fixed rate loans offer certainty of rate but are a double-edged sword. There is no guarantee the rate will be competitive compared to the current variable interest rate at any time during the fixed rate period. Never fix your home loan if you believe any of the following events may occur during the fixed rate period:

1. You will sell your property and repay the loan in full
2. You will want to repay a large lump sum
3. You believe the variable rates may decrease
4. There is usually no redraw option during the fixed rate term, so if you want this feature, look at variable rate loans

Are Fees Illegal?

Financial institutions in Australia are charging hundreds of millions of dollars in fees each year. The fees are outlined in the legal agreements all borrowers sign. However, it is important to understand the financial institutions are legally allowed only to recover actual costs; they can't be seen to be charging a fee as a penalty. Nor can a fee be charged that has not previously been disclosed, so check your loan contract and challenge any fee that is not documented.

Recently, due to consumer protests and the work of Choice and the Consumer Action Law Centre in Victoria, a number of financial institutions reduced or removed some fees. Generally the fees have related to transactional type accounts, but many fees, such as dishonour fees, also relate to loan accounts.

If you are charged a fee, you can dispute it by claiming:

1. The charge is excessive.

2. The charges are out of proportion and unconscionable in comparison with the lender's costs in providing the service. For example, a fee of $20 charged for a dishonour is unconscionable if the lender's costs in managing the dishonour are a few dollars.

3. There is a clear difference in the bargaining power between the financial institution and you as an individual consumer. As a consumer, you had no opportunity to negotiate the terms of your loan contract with the lender and, in any case, would have no ability to change any of the terms imposing fees and charges.

A written complaint outlining the above will in most cases result in a refund, but be aware: your lender will most likely do this as an exception and will not refund a second occurrence!

SUMMARY: Fees are becoming a bigger burden on you as a borrower. You should take into account the fees you will have to pay over the life of the loan. More often than not, that low interest rate will be hiding high fees!

Chapter 5:
The lending life cycle stages

∙∙∙

In this Chapter:

➤ Lending life cycle stages
➤ How long will it take to get my loan approved?

∙∙∙

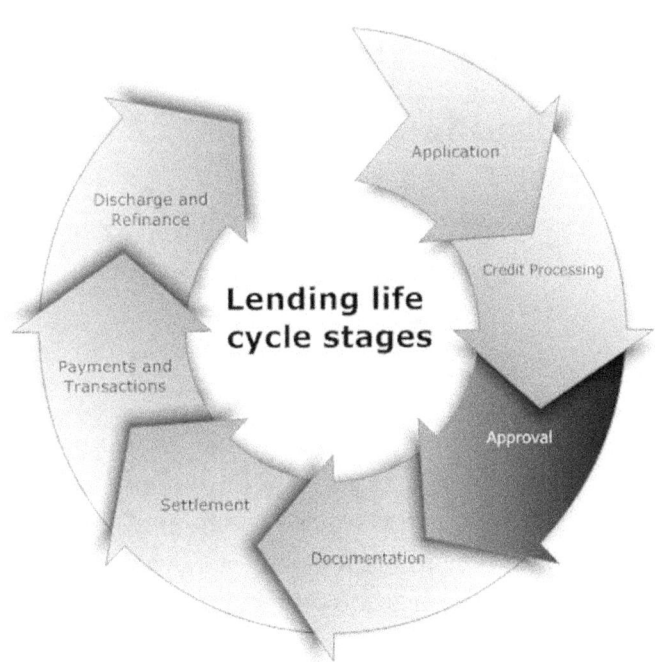

The lending life cycle is broken into the following key stages, from application to discharge and refinance.

Application: the processes around applying for a loan

Credit Processing: the lender's processes to evaluate your application

Approval: the processes the lender undertakes to approve your loan

Documentation: the processes the lender goes through to provide you with the loan documentation

Settlement: the processes the lender undertakes to provide the loan funds to you

Repayment and Transactions: the processes you and the lender go through to make and record the ongoing payments and transactions on the loan

Discharge and Refinance: the steps taken by you and the lender to repay the loan, either by you finding a new lender and refinancing, or by repaying the loan with your own funds, or the sale of the property

When you refinance a loan, the process begins again at application.

Let's look at each stage in a brief overview.

Stage 1: Application

At this stage you have chosen a lender and a loan type, most likely by comparing a number of options. You have confirmed how much you need to borrow and when you need the money. This is really important, especially if you are purchasing a new property. You will now have submitted an application either directly with the lender or through a mortgage broker.

Stage 2: Credit Processing

The credit processing stage is where the lender makes the decision whether to approve or decline your application. Generally, most lenders use a credit scoring system to confirm you meet their requirements, along with a credit check and a valuation of the property you are buying or refinancing.

Stage 3: Approval

The approval stage involves the lender confirming you are approved, the interest rate you will be charged, and any fees that will be applicable.

Stage 4: Documentation

The documentation stage involves you receiving and signing the loan documents, including the mortgage and any other forms the lender may require.

Stage 5: Settlement

The settlement stage involves the lender advancing the money and the loan commencing. You will pay any government fees and charges, and if purchasing the property, the title will be changed to your name. The lender's mortgage will be registered against the property title.

Stage 6: Payments and Transactions

During this stage you manage your loan, making repayments and other transactions. You will be charge interest and fees and receive statements and notices from the lender.

Stage 7: Discharge and Refinance

At some point in the future you will want to sell your home to buy a new property, or just change lenders. This process is called a refinance. The first step is to have your new loan approved, then ask your existing lender to discharge their mortgage. Your existing lender will provide you with a payout figure. This is the amount you need to pay the lender to close the loan.

How long will it take to get your loan approved?

While there is no industry-wide service standard for loan approvals, generally your home loan approval usually takes around two weeks. The process goes through a number of steps, as follows:

Conditional Approval: You have completed the application with the lender and your loan is approved in principal. This approval is subject to a number of conditions being met and additional documentation being provided. Usually these conditions are confirmation of your employment and income and a valuation of the property. In this step the lender has completed a credit check and confirmed serviceability based on the information you have provided. However, the lender has generally not verified this information and may be waiting on other evidence to move forward, such as evidence of deposit, loan repayment history, details of any adverse defaults in your credit check file, or LMI approval. A conditional approval may be provided in as little as a few minutes or as long as forty-eight hours.

Unconditional Approval: By this step the lender will have verified all your application information (employment, income, credit check, property valuation, and LMI if applicable). This can take some time, as the lender will need to contact your employer and complete a valuation of the property. These processes can usually be completed within a maximum of two weeks but usually within a five to six day period.

Pre-approval: This is the process of applying for a loan before you have found the property you wish to purchase. If you requested a pre-approval, the lender will complete all the verification steps other than the property valuation and LMI application. Pre-approval gives you the opportunity to confirm how much the lender is willing and able to offer you as a loan. However, you must remember that the property valuation is the key to determining how much you can borrow. You may have a pre-approval for a set amount, but that is still subject to the valuation of the security property.

In recent years lenders have been able to provide conditional approval very quickly, often within twenty-four hours, and in some cases within just a few hours. The unconditional approval still requires verification of key details, including a valuation of the property. While some lenders are using automated valuations, many still require a valuer to go to the property. This can mean waiting for the vendor of the property to allow access and another day or two for the report to be written.

Chapter 6:

The Application

• •

In this Chapter:

➤ The application
➤ Proof of identity
➤ Evidence of income

• •

Having some insider knowledge of the application process will allow you to understand what the lender wants and give you a better chance of getting your loan approved faster.

There are three key stages in applying for a loan:

1. Completing the application form
2. Proof of identity
3. Evidence of income

Described below is the general market practice for a prudent mortgage lender.

Completing the Application Form

When you require money to purchase a new property or refinance the debt on a property you already own, you will be applying for a completely new loan. The application process is an information-collection and processing task for the lender. The lender will want to understand who you are, what you want to use the loan funds for, whether you can afford to repay the loan, and the value of the security property offered. This will allow the lender to complete its credit assessment. All lenders have a credit policy that sets out their internal guidelines for lending. These policies cover:

- The type of borrowers that are acceptable
- What is an acceptable credit history for the borrower
- The maximum loan amount (based on the income and expenses of the borrowers)
- The maximum loan to value ratio (the percentage borrowed against the value of the security property)
- The type of properties that are acceptable as security
- The maximum loan term
- The interest rates, fees, and charges that will apply

Each lender's credit policy will be slightly different. Credit risk is a complex field that is constantly changing. Lenders face challenges in balancing market share against credit quality and ensuring borrowers can afford to repay loans.

Generally, you contact a sales representative of the lender and arrange a meeting to discuss the application. At this interview, the lender's representative will generally complete a needs analysis designed to:

- Confirm the reason you are applying for the loan (i.e., to purchase a new property or refinance an existing property)
- Identify the applicants (and guarantors, if applicable)
- Confirm the product required to match the applicant's needs (i.e., fixed or variable rate loan, product features such as redraw, etc.)
- Confirm the pricing (interest rate, fees, and charges)
- Confirm the maximum loan amount

- Confirm the important deadlines, including the date that funds are required (the settlement date)
- Make a final recommendation to either approve or decline the application

The interview may be conducted in several ways, including:

1. In person at the lender's offices/branch
2. In person at your home by the lender's representative
3. By telephone directly with the lender
4. In person with a mortgage broker (either at your home or at the broker's offices)
5. Over the web (at either the lender's or a broker's website)

In the current lending market, you generally shop around for the best deal or seek a mortgage broker to help you find an acceptable loan.

&**TIP:** Be prepared at the interview. It will make the process a lot simpler and quicker. Below is a list of useful things to have on hand:

- Know how much you wish to borrow, and make sure you have provided for costs like stamp duty and fees in the total loan amount required.
- Know why you are applying for the loan. Is it for a property you intend to live in, or will the loan be for investment purposes, such as buying an investment property or shares?
- Have a complete list of all your assets and liabilities (what you owe and what you own).
- Know your before- and after-tax income and have evidence of it with you.
- Give the interviewer clear deadlines for approval.
- Have details of the property being offered as security, including its full address and description.
- If buying a property, provide copies of the contract of sale.

- If refinancing, have your last six months of loan statements showing your repayment history.

- Have photo identification for all applicants and guarantors (at least a driver's licence) as well as other identification like a credit card or birth certificate.

- Provide the address, phone, and e-mail details of the solicitor or conveyancer acting for you (if applicable).

- If possible, have photocopies of these documents ready to give to the interviewer (but remember to have the originals on hand as well).

- Have a list of questions ready to ask.

The first step in the application process is the application form. This may be a physical paper form, an electronic form completed on a computer (by the lender's representative), a web form you complete, or a simple list of questions asked by a call centre. This form will be completed at the initial interview. This document is officially completed by the borrower and details all your personal information and your financial position. If someone else completes the form for you, make sure the information contained in the form is correct before signing the document!

It's critical to fill in the application form fully and answer all questions, as this is the key document that the lender will use to process your application. Simple mistakes here can cause major delays, or even result in your application being declined!

Below is a comprehensive list of the information collected in the application form and what it is generally used for by the lender:

- **Borrower's full name and address:** Used by the lender to identify the borrower for credit checks and legal requirements. Also to address letters to the borrower and for creation of the legal documents.

- **How long you have lived at your current address:** Used to assist the lender in the process of identifying the borrower. Also used by some lenders as an indication of an applicant's stability.

- **Contact Details:** Generally used to contact the borrower. However, some lenders use this information in the assessment process using a system called credit scoring. Not including contact details like your home telephone number can be detrimental to your credit score.

- **Employment Details:** The lender will use this information along with your proof of income to calculate your ability to repay the loan and meet your day-to-day living expenses.

- **Property Details:** The lender will use this information, firstly to confirm the property is acceptable as a security in terms of the lender's credit policy, and secondly to arrange a valuation.

- **Assets and Liabilities Statement:** This is a list of what you own (assets) and what you owe (liabilities). Assets are things like properties, cars, boats, shares, cash, personal possessions, etc. Liabilities are things like loans, credit cards, store cards, overdrafts, etc. The lender will need to know the approximate value of each asset and the balances and required repayments of each liability. Lenders generally need to see an excess of assets over liabilities, meaning you must own more than you owe.

Generally, loan application forms range between ten and fifteen pages. While an application form can seem quite a long document, on average it takes less than half an hour to complete. Lenders and their representatives will generally assist you in completing the form. Many application forms are now electronic.

✒**TIP:** Remember to complete the application form in full. Most lenders now use complex credit scoring to evaluate your application. If you forget to list all your contact telephone numbers (home, work, mobile, and fax if applicable) this may be seen by the lender as a negative. Basically, if lenders put a question on the application form, it's because that information is important to them!

🖎**LEGAL ISSUES:** Lenders collect, store, and use your personal information. However, they must adhere to the Privacy Act, which requires them to store your personal information securely and not to give or sell it without your approval. You also have the right to see all the information they hold on you and make any corrections.

Proof of Identity

In Australia, all financial institutions formally identify their applicants, so you will have to provide proof of identity. It's a major legal requirement that you can't avoid.

There are strong legal requirements placed on lenders under the Anti-Money Laundering and Counter-Terrorism Financing Act. All banks, non-bank lenders, credit unions, and building societies who offer loans have to adhere to the act's minimum requirements. The past standard for borrower identification was the one hundred point verification scheme established under the Financial Transaction Reports Act 1988 (FTRA).

Generally, the lending industry still follows the FTRA requirements to identify applicants by collecting different forms of identification, each of which is allocated a points value. Applicants are considered to be satisfactorily identified when the total points value of their IDs reaches or exceeds one hundred points. Documents or evidence are split into two categories, primary or secondary. Primary documents score seventy points, but only one can be used in the identification process. Secondary documents or evidence score a range of points from forty to twenty-five each.

The Anti-Money Laundering and Counter-Terrorism Financing Act introduced the concept of "know your customer," which requires the lender to not only identify the borrower but also collect additional information such as full name, date of birth, and address.

Generally speaking, the most acceptable forms of identification are passports, birth certificates, and citizenship certificates as the primary document. Drivers licences, Medicare cards, and credit cards act as the supporting secondary documents.

The application will not be processed without all applicants being adequately identified. If you already have an account with the lender, this requirement will usually be waived. However, the lender may still complete separate identity checks, often electronically.

Evidence of Income

The lender has an obligation to satisfy itself that an applicant can afford to repay the loan, and will complete an assessment based on the income and payment obligations of the applicant. The lender's representative will insist on evidence of income in the form of pay slips, letters from employers, or bank statements. Some lenders will want to see copies of the latest tax return and assessment or group certificate from all applicants.

Some types of loans do not require evidence of income, or only limited information in the form of a declaration. These loans are known in the lending industry as Low Doc or No Doc, meaning no documentary proof of income was provided. Such Low Doc loan applications will require the applicant to either sign a declaration that states the applicant's income and that they can make the required loan repayments (known as a declaration of income and affordability). In No Doc cases, a form simply states that the applicants believe they can make the required repayments (known as a declaration of affordability only). The National Consumer Credit Protection Act has strong requirements for lenders to prove applicants can make the loan repayments without financial hardship. This may mean that No Doc loans may disappear from the market, and that Low Doc loans will require some form of evidence of actual income.

The application can progress without evidence of income, but unconditional approval cannot be expected without it. Lenders are now taking a more active interest in confirming income, and many now call the employer directly to confirm income.

SUMMARY: The application process usually involves an interview with the lender's representative. An application form will be completed and signed by the applicants and any guarantors. Evidence of identification and income will need to be provided.

The application will then be sent for credit assessment. If you have provided all the information and proof of identity and income, the lender will be in a good position to complete the credit assessment. If you haven't, you can expect a call from a credit manager, and possibly a delay in getting your loan approved.

Chapter 7:
Credit Assessment and Approval

• •

In this Chapter:

➤ The four Cs of credit
➤ Character

    ➤ Types of borrowers

    ➤ Non-resident borrowers

    ➤ Your credit file

➤ Capacity

    ➤ Borrowers of convenience

➤ Collateral

    ➤ Mortgage insurance

    ➤ Deposit

➤ Conditions
➤ Electronic Credit scoring systems
➤ Approval

• •

All loan applications undergo credit assessment before being approved. If the application meets the requirements of the lender (and mortgage insurer, if applicable) the loan is approved. However, this is an involved process that can take some time to complete. The application commonly goes through four assessment steps, known in the industry as the four Cs of credit.

The Four Cs of Credit

- **Character**
- **Capacity**
- **Collateral**
- **Conditions**

The lender will use the information contained in the application and the supporting documents (identification documents, proof of income, etc.) to arrive at an initial decision as to whether to proceed with the application. If encouraged to proceed, the lender will seek further information on the credit history of the applicants and guarantors and have a formal valuation of the security property undertaken.

It is very important to fully complete the application form and supply all the supporting information up front; it means the credit assessment can proceed without delay.

Character

Your past credit history and financial management history are critical to the credit assessment process. The lender will evaluate your employment history and stability of residence to form an opinion of your willingness to meet the required repayments. The lender is looking at your application form to see how honest you have been. Have you listed all your debts? Is the value of your assets in line with what would be expected of an applicant of your age, line of work, and employment history?

If the loan is required to refinance an existing loan, lenders will ask to see the last six months of statements for the loan being refinanced. This is so they can see if all the required repayments were made on time. Again, they are looking at your payment history for an indication of your willingness to meet future obligations.

While the application form provides a lot of key information, the lender will make use of a credit file agency as well.

Types of Borrowers

While most home loans are in the individual names of the borrowers, other entities can be borrowers for the purpose of lending:

Companies: Companies can borrow in their own names, and this is common for investment purposes. The lender will usually require all directors and shareholders (excluding notional directors) to provide unconditional joint and several personal guarantees. You may choose to have a company own the property for tax reasons, or you may be going into a complex investment with other people.

Trusts: Trusts can also borrow. This is useful if you wish to establish a family trust to move personal assets out of your name and into the name of a trust. Again, when the trustee is a company, the lender will usually require all directors to provide unconditional joint and personal guarantees. The lender will have standard requirements for all trusts, including guarantees to be given by all adult beneficiaries. The lender will want to see the trust deed and have it reviewed.

Non-Resident Borrowers: A non-resident borrower is deemed to be any person without permanent residency status in Australia, or any person who resides and is employed in another country.

New Zealand citizens living and working in New Zealand or permanent residents of New Zealand are usually considered residents of Australia by most lenders and are not treated as non-residents.

Lenders will allow non-residents to borrow for investment purposes. The property must be used for residential investment and must be rented. Also, non-resident borrowers purchasing a property in Australia must obtain written approval from the Foreign Investment Review Board. The lender will require a copy of the approval prior to approving any loan.

Your Credit File

A major part of reviewing your character is to check your credit history. This is done by requesting a credit file. In Australia there are two credit file agencies, Veda Advantage and Dun & Bradstreet. Veda Advantage is the credit file agency most often used for personal lending. It was formerly known as Baycorp Advantage, which, in turn, was previously known as the CRAA (Credit Reference Association of Australia).

Dun & Bradstreet have specialised in credit files for businesses and are more often used in the telecommunication market. Both companies hold credit reports on individual borrowers in Australia and New Zealand. The report lists the number and type of previous credit checks, court judgments, and defaults. The listing generally holds all enquiries made over the last seven years and all defaults over the last ten years.

Credit files contain a history of loan applications made where a credit check has been requested, payment defaults, bankruptcies, etc. In the credit assessment process, the lender will take into account the number of loan enquiries and defaults. Some have strict guidelines on the number of enquiries within predefined periods. For example, the lender may have rules around enquiries within the last three months. All is not lost if you have a busy credit enquiry history; just be ready to answer some questions from the lender about the loans you actually have at the moment.

Lenders are becoming more focused on this aspect of the application. If you are a new borrower, lenders must use the information they find in the application form and credit file to get an understanding of what you have done in the past. This is the best indicator of how you will manage the new loan in the future.

✒**TIP:** If you are shopping around at different lenders for the best deal, be aware that you should not apply to each of them, as they will all complete a credit report enquiry. This may affect your chances of getting a loan, as your credit file may show numerous recent enquires and will look busy.

It's a good idea to know what's on your credit file. It can prevent nasty surprises, like disputed mobile phone contract defaults, from ruining your application!

You can request a free copy of your credit file from Veda Advantage at any time. Simply download an application directly from their website, and your file will be posted to you in about three weeks. They also offer a premium service where the credit file is e-mailed to you for a fee. Other services include a tracking service that informs you of all enquiries made on your file.

If you find an error in your credit file, lodge a dispute with the lender who has the ability to remove errors.

Capacity

Capacity is your ability to repay the loan over the loan's term. Most people will repay the loan using income from wages, salary, or investments. The lender reviews your income. The lender will verify the annual wages or salary amount, usually by requesting evidence such as a pay slip. The evidence of income collected with the application form is reviewed to ensure the income stated in the application form is the same. It is common market practice for the lender to test your income in a number of ways. Generally, the lender will want to see a number of different documents to prove your income. This will usually include your two most recent pay slips, a letter from your employer, and/or bank statements showing the regular payments coming in. The lender is very likely to telephone your employer directly to confirm the income as well.

The lender also looks at your assets and liabilities statement to confirm that you have a surplus of assets over liabilities. Generally, the greater the surplus the better, as this demonstrates financial strength— you have collected more assets than debts.

Once income is confirmed, your serviceability is calculated. Serviceability is your ability to service (repay) all proposed debts, as well as your living expenses, out of your normal income. Commonly the lender will use a "Net Surplus Ratio" calculator, or NSR. This serviceability test is normally created in Microsoft Excel. The spreadsheet calculates the applicant's income details, along with living expenses and loan repayments, to calculate a ratio of income to total expenses. The ratio is normally expressed as 1:1 (i.e., the minimum is $1 of income for each $1 of debt repayments, after living expenses).

Example: Mr. Smith applies for a home loan of $150,000 with an interest rate of 7.99 percent. His annual before-tax income is $85,000 (excluding superannuation). He has an existing credit card with a limit of $5,000 and a car loan of $15,000 with repayments of $299 per month.

Annual Income		
Salary/Wages		$85,000
Tax on Income		$22,375
Net Income	A	$62,625
Annual Living Expenses and Loan/Credit Card Repayments		
Living Expenses	B	$11,289
Repayment on New Loan	C	$15,228
Repayment on Car Loan	D	$3,588
Minimum Credit Card Repayments (Generally 3% of the actual card limit per month multiplied by 12 months)	E	$1,800
Total		$31,905
Net Surplus Calculation		
Net Income less Living Expenses (A-B)	F	$51,336
Total Debt repayments (New Loan, Car Loan and Credit Card Repayments) (C+D+E)	G	$20,615
Net Income divided by Total Debits Repayments (NSR Ratio) (F/G)		2.29:1

The lender will make an estimate of Mr. Smith's living expenses—in this case, $11,289. This estimate will change depending on the type of applicant. Thus, living expenses increase for couples and for applicants with dependants. The lender usually bases the living expenses on the Melbourne Institute of Applied Economics and Social Research's poverty line analysis, which sets the official cost of living in Australia.

This means that after paying his living expenses, Mr. Smith has $2.29 of income for each $1 of debt repayment. He would pass this NSR test, as his NSR is better than 1:1.

Some loan types don't require actual evidence of income. Often called Low Doc loans, these loans require you to either state or certify your income and your ability to afford loan repayments in a legal document, usually a Low Doc application form. In other cases, you are not required to disclose your income at all. When you make an income declaration, it will be tested in an NSR.

Borrowers of Convenience

A borrower of convenience is defined as a borrower that is added to the loan application to provide additional income to increase service-ability and/or security to allow the loan to be approved. However, this borrower does not receive any tangible benefit from the loan transaction itself.

Lenders generally require borrowers to have a beneficial interest in the loan transaction, either by way of joint ownership of the property and/or dependence on the mortgagor in a marital or de facto relationship.

Most lenders will not accept an additional borrower being added to a loan simply to provide income support for serviceability, or to provide added security for another party to purchase a property.

Lenders prefer guarantees that clearly set out the liability the guarantor has provided. However, guarantor's incomes are not usually allowed to be included in serviceability.

Collateral

The term collateral refers to the security property that is mortgaged to support the loan. Lenders will analyse the property to ensure it meets their credit policies. Lenders are looking for quality properties and will exclude properties that do not meet the minimum standard. Some common exclusions are:

- Properties that are damaged or under construction and can't be lived in
- Properties that are considered "special purpose" (i.e., retirement homes or serviced apartments)
- Properties under fifty square metres
- Heritage-listed properties

- Large farms (farm lending is generally considered commercial lending)

- Commercial properties (buildings used as shops or offices)

In most cases, the lender will have a valuation undertaken to confirm the fair market value of the property. The lender's valuer will provide a written valuation, which the lender will use to calculate the LVR.

Some lenders have a "No Val" policy in which the purchase price of the security property is accepted as the market value. This No Val process was created in part to speed up the approval process and was also used for low LVR loans (less than 80 percent in almost all cases). Most lenders have removed their No Val policies in recent times, mostly due to bad press regarding two-tier marketing.

The valuation will be addressed to the lender and its LMI provider for their own use and benefit. It is not regarded as the property of the borrower, even if the borrower has paid the valuation fee.

The valuation report provides details of the security property, its current physical condition, and relative market value compared to similar properties sold in the same area or similar areas. It is important to note that if the property being valued is a unit, the valuer may not be able to use property sales in the same block for the comparison. Most lenders see this as possibly risky due to some property investors' marketing methods.

The main areas that will be evaluated are:

- Valuation amount

- Condition of the property (particularly any adverse comments from the valuer)

- Population density

- Comparative sales information

- Post code (used by LMI providers)

There are other types of valuation, including progress inspections for construction loans, when the valuer will confirm that a certain value of work has been carried out at a particular stage of construction.

Valuations are performed in a number of different ways. A full valuation requires the valuer to visit the security property and complete an inspection. This is generally the most expensive form of valuation. Lenders may choose other, less expensive methods, such as desktop or automated valuations. Both of these valuations rely on statistical data (provided by land title offices) without an actual site visit being made.

Valuers

Valuers are instructed and paid by the lender but may have direct contact with you. When the property to be mortgaged is being acquired as part of the loan, the valuer will contact the real estate agent and arrange an inspection. When the loan is a refinance, the valuer will most likely contact you directly to arrange an inspection. The lending industry is constantly developing new and better electronic solutions, and valuations are increasingly being completed using Automated Valuation Models (AVMs), where statistical sales data only is used and the valuer may not actually inspect the property. This type of valuation is often undertaken when the LVR on the loan is below 50 percent of the estimated value.

Loan to Value Ratio (LVR)

The LVR is important to the lender, as it is the value of the security property being loaned to you. Usually lenders will advance up to 80 percent of the property's value without LMI. For the applicant to borrow a greater proportion of the property's value, LMI will usually be required.

Example: Mrs. Smith is purchasing a property for $600,000 and is seeking a loan of $300,000. The valuation confirms the security property has fair market value of $600,000, so the LVR is calculated by dividing the loan amount by the valuation expressed as a percentage ($300,000 divided by $600,000 = LVR of 50 percent).

Lender's Mortgage Insurance

If you are looking to borrow more than 80 percent of your property's value, you will need LMI. This insurance protects the lender against loss should you default on payment of your loan. While mortgage insurers do not directly fund or make loans, they allow lenders to provide a higher loan amount to you by providing an insurance policy for the lender against possible losses. Mortgage insurance is usually used by balance-sheet lenders such as banks to allow for a higher loan amount. Policies can allow for lending above 80 percent.

TIP: It is important to note that the insurance policy does not cover the borrower's liability. If you default, you will still be liable.

Deposit

Your deposit is a key indicator of your financial capacity, and the lender takes it into account when completing its credit assessment. The higher your deposit the better, as this means you will own more of the property and will be less likely to default. Lenders view deposits in a number of ways:

Equity in existing properties: If you already have a property, the lender will look at the current market valuation, less any debt, to establish your equity. Lenders look favourably on borrower equity, as it shows you have a track record of maintaining or improving an asset.

Genuine savings: These are savings held in your name and accumulated in a savings or investment account for three or more months. Usually you will need to provide evidence that you have a savings history by providing supporting documents such as bank statements showing regular deposits. This shows the lender you are disciplined and can afford to make regular payments.

Non-Genuine savings: This generally means a deposit you have received as a gift or from the sale of other non-financial assets. If you received a gift, the lender will usually require a gift certificate from the person who provided the gift. The gift certificate states you do not have to repay the gift at any stage, therefore reassuring the lender you have not actually borrowed the deposit.

Rent as evidence of savings: Some lenders are now looking at rental payments as evidence of a regular ability to make a payment. This is, however, a very limited option offered in limited instances.

Your deposit is important to the lender, as it evidences your financial position while providing a history of progressive savings.

When the lender has reviewed the valuation, and in cases where LMI is required, applied for, and approved by the insurer, the loan can move on to the final stage of the approval process.

Conditions

Conditions refer to the lender's internal policies and product rules. Conditions are generally product-specific, such as maximum loan amounts, maximum LVRs, terms, and repayments. The conditions of a loan set out how the loan will operate.

Electronic Credit Scoring Systems

It's becoming common for lenders to use computer-based credit scoring systems in their credit analysis. These systems take in the information from the application form and produce a score based on the information you provide.

These systems allocate points to you based on your current financial position and history, along with the contact information provided. A credit scoring model might give positive points to an applicant who has lived in the same residence for the last three to five years, while giving negative points to applicants whose residency is less than three years. These models are complex and rely on the information in the application form, which is why it's important that you complete the application form in full. These systems don't like blanks!

Approval

When the credit assessment has been completed and the lender is satisfied that you can meet your obligation to repay the loan and that the security property offered is satisfactory, they will usually approve the loan.

Generally, the lender will issue a letter of offer. This will be sent out with the terms of the loan prior to the actual loan documents being issued.

At this point the interest rate, fees, and charges will be confirmed. Repayments will be calculated and documents drawn up.

✒**TIP:** The top five ways to ensure your loan is approved quickly and with as little fuss as possible:
1. Save more; borrow less
2. Increase your income
3. Decrease your existing debt
4. Close unwanted credit cards or store cards
5. Keep a clean credit history

Chapter 8:

Settlement and Loan Management

••

In this Chapter:

➤ Things you need for settlement

  ➤ Building insurance

  ➤ Signing and returning documents

➤ Settlement letter

➤ Access methods

➤ Transactions

  ➤ Statements

➤ Variations

  ➤ Loan structures

  ➤ Further advance/additional advances/principal increase

  ➤ Consents

  ➤ Repayment holidays/parental leave period

  ➤ Portability

➤ Disputes with your lender

  ➤ Industry bodies

  ➤ Financial Services Ombudsman (FSO)

➤ Paying off a Loan
➤ Discharging
➤ Refinancing
    ➤ Why refinance?

• •

Things You Need for Settlement

There are a few final steps before you can settle your new loan, and several things you will need:

Building Insurance

You will need to insure the property being offered as security and also have the lender's name recorded on the policy as mortgagee.

If the property is a strata title unit, you may need to get the lender a copy of the policy that is held for the entire unit block. The lender's name will not necessarily need to be recorded as it is with a house.

Some lenders will ask you to provide a fresh copy of your property's insurance at each renewal.

Signing and Returning Documents

Prior to settlement you will have signed the loan documents, mortgage, and other documents and returned them to the lender or its panel solicitor.

At settlement, the loan funds will be drawn and the lender or its solicitor will make out bank cheques to either the vendor or the outgoing mortgagee.

Settlement is reliant on a number of factors, including:

- Vacant possession of the property—if you are purchasing a property, the occupants must move out before settlement

- A discharge of mortgage, if a refinance

- In any case, the property must be covered by building replacement insurance, as this is a key requirement of all lenders

- Any fees payable to the lender that have not already been paid will be deducted from the proceeds of the loan

If you have a conveyancer or solicitor acting on your behalf, he or she will arrange for settlement and advise you of any additional costs you may need to pay. If you are purchasing a property, he or she will inform the council and have the rates records updated. The same is true for strata managed properties.

Once settlement has occurred, the lender will normally issue a welcome letter detailing the actual interest rate, repayments, repayment frequencies, and terms.

Settlement of the loan is really only the beginning. Settlement (sometimes called drawdown) is when the loan funds are released. It is the point from which interest starts to accrue and the parties become bound by the rights and obligations of the loan contract.

Settlement Letter

Most lenders will issue the borrowers a settlement letter shortly after the loan is settled. This communicates key information about the loan, such as:

- Repayments: the amount and frequency required
- Interest rates: the prevailing rate and whether it is fixed or variable
- Term: the length of any fixed or interest-only term and the total loan term

Alternatively, the lender may arrange a direct call to you to discuss the setup of repayments and access methods.

Access Methods

As part of the settlement letter, or separately at about the same time, the lender will provide you with the details of the various methods available to access or operate your loan facility. Generally speaking, there are three common access methods:

1. In person, through over-the-counter withdrawals, deposits, and enquiries at the lender's branch. This is becoming less common as banks close down local branches and increase fees at branches to encourage you to use telephone or Internet banking.
2. By telephone. Call centres offer basic assistance to borrowers. However, some lenders outsource call centres, and you may end up speaking to someone in another country!
3. Internet or telephone banking. The lender will issue a login code and password. This allows you to access services over the Internet, or by telephone, using an interactive voice response system (IVR). Such services include:

   - Account balances

   - Transaction listings

   - Additional payment requests

   - Redraw requests to nominated accounts, by BPAY or Pay Anyone

SMS banking is now being offered by some lenders, allowing access to many of the same services directly from any mobile phone.

Most lenders are now also building custom applications for smart phones and tablet computers, to allow for mobile Internet banking.

Transactions

Once settled, the loan enters the transaction phase where repayments are made, interest is charged, and statements issued. Transactions can be:

1. Credits

   - Direct debit repayments: monthly, fortnightly, weekly, or one-off

   - Salary credit: the direct payment of part or all of your wages to the loan account

- Electronic credit: other direct payments to the loan account such as rental payments, dividend payments, etc.

- Over-the-counter deposits (by cash or cheque)

2. Debits

- Interest

- Fees

- Redraws by:

  ○ Telephone, Internet banking, or SMS Banking, including internal transfers and transfers to linked bank accounts

  ○ BPAY

  ○ Pay Anyone—usually made by using Internet banking; the payment is sent to the recipient's bank account using the bank account number

  ○ Inward Direct debit—usually for or any regular utility bill, such as electricity

3. Informational

- Rate changes: usually changes in the variable rate or a convert to or from a fixed rate

- Interest savings estimates for offset accounts

Statements

The lender will provide you with a statement of account. By law, this must occur at least twice a year, usually at 30 June and 31 December. Lenders often provide statements more frequently.

By their nature, some lending products require more regular statements. For example, lines of credit and interest-only loans commonly have monthly statements.

Almost all lenders offer transaction listings by telephone or Internet banking and will charge a fee to produce an ad hoc or out-of-cycle statement or reprint a previously issued statement.

This can be very costly, as you generally need to have six months of statements to allow for a refinance. So remember to keep your statements in a safe place or risk being charged a fee for each statement page reprinted.

Some lenders are now offering "paper-less" statements were instead of receiving a statement in the post you receive the statement as an email attachment, or logon to internet banking to view the statement.

Variations

Variations are changes made to the loan contract after settlement, such as when you request a change to the loan structure; an increase in the loan amount (commonly called a further advance or an additional advance); or when you request access to the certificate of title to perform a change, such as a subdivision or any other consent.

Loan Structure Variations

Changes to loan structure relate to requests to amend the type of loan, for example, converting from principal and interest repayments to interest-only repayments. These changes usually involve the lender providing you with a legal document that contractually changes the loan. Other examples of a structure change are:

- Converting from a variable interest rate to fixed rate
- Converting from a term loan to a line of credit
- Establishing an additional split account and/or transferring part of the existing loan to a new account

Further Advances/Additional Advances/ Principal Increases

The most common variation is the further advance, sometimes called an additional advance or a principal increase. This is simply a request by you for an increase in the limit of the loan.

In many ways, this process is very similar to the application process. You will be required to complete an application form, and there will be a credit assessment. A valuation may be required, and a credit check will be undertaken. If the application is approved, you will be required to enter into a revised loan contract.

Consents

A consent occurs when the lender agrees to vary the loan contract or when there is any change to a property's title for things like:

- Substitution of security property: when you sell a property and buy another at the same time

- Partial release of security property: when you have mortgaged more than one property as security for the loan and may have sold one of the properties

- Addition of a security property: when you borrow more to buy a new property and add the new property as additional security for the (increased) loan

- Consent to a second or subsequent mortgage: when you take out an additional loan with another lender using the same security property

- Subdivision of the security property: when you get approval to separate the title to your property into multiple (smaller) lots of land with separate titles

Most consents will require legal documents to be drawn up. The lender will charge a fee and possibly other legal costs.

Repayment Holidays/Parental Leave Period

A repayment holiday or a parental leave period is a feature of some loans that allows you to stop making regular repayments for a short time. The repayment holiday terms range from three to six months. The lender will usually charge a fee, and while repayments are not required, interest is still calculated and charged. This means that during the repayment holiday your loan will capitalise and grow in size.

There are two forms of repayment holiday: when you have made additional payments to the loan and will use these additional payments to cover the holiday period, or when the loan limit will be increased by the interest you will not pay.

Example: Say you have prepaid your loan and decide to take a repayment holiday. If your loan was for $250,000 with an interest rate of 7.49 percent, your repayment would be $1,746.32 per month. To allow for a three-month payment holiday, you would need to repay and additional $5,238 over the twelve months prior to the payment holiday at $444 per month. This would allow for a payment holiday without the loan growing, and as the prepayment is made over a year, you would actually have made a small interest saving.

If you don't prepay, a repayment holiday will increase the limit of your loan. Using the same basic loan details as above, you would increase your loan by $4,641 in interest over the repayment holiday.

✦ **WARNING:** As a general rule, it's never a good idea to capitalise interest!

Portability

Portability is a feature of some loans that allows you to transfer the loan to a new property. So if you sell your home and purchase a new home, the loan transfers to the new property. There are usually a number of conditions around this, such as simultaneous settlement (when the sale and purchase of the properties occurs on the same day) and the usual credit approval.

Some lenders will allow you a limited amount of time to find a new property after selling your home. The lender will keep the loan open. You will still make repayments, and they will hold the settlement funds from the sale of the property.

Portability is a good product feature if you have entered into a fixed rate, as you can save yourself from break costs related to repaying any fixed rate loan.

Industry Bodies

The mortgage industry has a number of industry bodies. Generally these organisations are split across the sector as either lenders (banks and mutuals) or broker associations. The banks and larger lenders are members of the Australian Bankers' Association and the Financial Services Ombudsman. The smaller lenders and brokers are members of the Mortgage & Finance Association of Australia (MFAA), the Finance Brokers Association of Australia (FBAA) and the Credit Ombudsman Services Limited.

Industry bodies support their members' interests and are often involved in providing an industry voice. This advice and advocacy contributes to the development of public policy on lending during consultations with government regarding industry reforms.

The industry bodies have strict codes of conduct and often act as an advocate for the borrower. They also provide lists of active members you can search to ensure the professional you are dealing with is accredited.

If you are using a lender or mortgage broker you have not heard of before, it's a good idea to check that they are accredited by a major industry body. Accreditation means they have reached a minimum level of industry knowledge and have adequate insurance to protect consumers.

Example organisations:

- Abacus (Australian mutuals covering mutual building societies, credit unions, and friendly societies) www.abacus.org.au

- Australian Bankers' Association
  www.bankers.ans.au

- Finance Brokers Association of Australia (FBAA) www.financebroker.com.au

- Mortgage & Finance Association of Australia (MFAA) www.mfaa.com.au

Disputes with Your Lender

While the lending industry is highly automated, people make mistakes, and you should dispute any fees and charges you do not believe you agreed to pay. It's important to complain in writing, as written complaints are taken more seriously and require a written response from the lender. Also tell the lender how you wish the dispute to be resolved (this will usually be a refund).

If you are not happy with the response from the lender, lodge a complaint with the industry body's dispute-resolution service. These dispute-resolution programs are usually free of charge and are independent; therefore, they are looking for the complaint to be resolved.

The mortgage industry has a number of industry bodies and an ombudsman to assist the public with complaints regarding industry members. These services are free to consumers and are approved and monitored by the Australian Securities and Investment Commission (ASIC). The ombudsman requires lenders to adhere to strict time frames for resolving customer complaints. The program sets out the process the lender must undertake to investigate the complaint, the minimum communication standards, and when the ombudsman can make a binding decision.

Financial Ombudsman Service

The Financial Ombudsman Service (FOS) is a free and independent dispute-resolution service for the banking and financial services industry. The FOS considers complaints about banks and their affiliates operating in Australia. Some non-banks are members, along with their affiliates.

The ombudsman is able to investigate disputes and make decisions that are binding on the financial services provider. The ombudsman's powers are set out in the Terms of Reference, available at their official website. As a general rule, the ombudsman can consider a dispute if:

- It is about a financial service provided by a member bank or an affiliate;
- The complainant is an individual or a small business; *and*

- The amount of loss the complainant is claiming is less than $280,000

There are some types of disputes that the ombudsman is unable to consider. These are set out in the Terms of Reference and include disputes about general policies such as interest rates, fees, and branch closures.

The FOS handled 23,790 new disputes in 2009–10, up six percent on the previous year. More than seven thousand of those disputes involved credit products, and the bulk of those (88 percent) related to consumer credit. The FOS also identified fifty-eight systemic issues in the finance industry during 2009–10. These issues were industry-wide and included processing delays resulting in costs to the account holder, failure to link eligible offset accounts, failure to cancel direct debits on request, and inadequate disclosure of fees and charges.

You can contact the FOS at www.fos.org.au

Credit Ombudsman Service Limited

The Credit Ombudsman Service Limited (COSL) is the external dispute-resolution scheme for the non-bank credit industry.

The COSL is a free and independent external dispute-resolution scheme. It provides consumers with an alternative to legal proceedings for resolving disputes with COSL members operating in the mortgage industry.

You can contact the COSL at www.creditombudsman.com.au

While the National Consumer Credit Protection Act (NCCP) is the core legislation for the lending industry, there are other important regulations, including the Electronic Funds Transfer Code of Conduct. This code sets limits on the extent to which an account holder can be held liable for unauthorised transactions, but an account holder may still be liable if they contribute to the loss.

It's very important to report to your lender any unusual transaction on your loan or transactional accounts as soon as you notice them. Waiting may limit your ability to receive a refund or to dispute the transaction.

Paying Off a Loan

A loan ends when it is repaid in full. The mortgage can then be discharged and removed from the certificate of title.

Discharging

If you have managed to fully repay your loan over its term, or early through making extra payments, good for you! You will get the deed to your property back and own it outright.

If you have sold a property held as security, your loan will still need to be fully repaid from the sale proceeds, but the deed to your property will pass to the new owner.

Refinancing

Repaying your loan with a new loan from a different lender is called refinancing.

Some lenders will attempt to retain your business. They may offer incentives for you to stay, or they may simply make it difficult to leave!

When discharging your loan, be aware that your lender may charge exit fees. You should take this into consideration when deciding to prepay your loan or sell your property.

Why Refinance?

There are a number of reasons to refinance your loan:

- Interest rate
- Features
- Debt consolidation
- You may be increasing your total borrowing and take the opportunity to look at a new lender

However, it is important not to refinance if:

- Your existing loan has high exit fees (if you have a fixed rate loan, you might also have to pay break costs)
- If you are unable to meet the existing repayments

Often people fall into the trap of refinancing when they don't need to. This may be because they are unaware that their existing lender can help them. This can result in additional costs, such as legal fees, registration fees, and exit fees from your existing lender.

Most lenders are happy to provide you with additional funds and can change your existing product to add new features. This is often much cheaper than refinancing.

Before you refinance, here are some important points to consider. As a borrower, ask yourself:

- Will I be better off with a new lender?
- Will the cost of moving outweigh any benefit from a reduced interest rate?
- Am I increasing my debt for the wrong reasons?

Questions to ask your existing lender:

- Can you save me money by reducing my interest rate or fees?
- Can you increase my loan limits?
- If I purchase additional services, do I receive any additional discounts or other benefits?

" So what happens if we can't meet our monthly mortgage repayments?"

Chapter 9:

When you miss a payment

....

In this Chapter:
➤ Default
➤ Repossession

....

If you find yourself unable to make your repayments, you should *seek help immediately! Contact a lawyer as quickly as you can!*

Default

Default usually occurs when you fail to make a repayment on time or when a repayment is dishonoured, leaving the loan over its documented credit limit. Lenders generally have three types of default events:

- Over-limit arrears: the loan balance is greater than the approved limit
- Missed payment arrears: a repayment has not been made when due (sometimes even if the loan is already paid ahead!)
- Technical default: a technical issue such as council rate arrears or failure to insure your property has occurred

The lender has entered into a legal contract with you, and the repayments of the loan form part of that agreement. Generally, the lender does not want to have to take possession of the security property and wants to assist you if you fall into difficulties.

Being in arrears is always stressful for you, and at times you can feel you have no options. There are, however, a number of things that you as a borrower can do to get out of arrears:

1. If you are making principal and interest repayments, convert the loan to interest only. Whilst your repayments should decrease immediately, the down side is you are not paying off any of the principal of the loan, but you may be able to pay the interest.
2. If you don't have a budget, now is the time to make one! There are a number of community organisations and online tools that can help you draw up a budget.
3. Did you know that you can access your superannuation to repay mortgage arrears? It's not a simple process, but you can apply to the Australian Securities and Investment Commission (ASIC). They will review your situation and have the power to make an order for payment. The maximum withdrawal per year is $36,000. This should be a last resort, but if this is the only way to save your home, then it is an option that must be considered.

4. Mortgage assistance schemes can provide short-term help. Such schemes exist in most states. For example, New South Wales residents experiencing temporary difficulties with their home loan repayments because of an unavoidable change in circumstances can apply for assistance. Some examples of temporary difficulties include unemployment, accident, illness, or other crisis. The assistance is paid directly to the lender to take the stress off families. There are, however, a lot of strict rules around these programs, so you need to contact the state government as quickly as possible to see if you qualify.

5. The National Consumer Credit Protection Act (NCCP) introduced the concept of hardship to the lending industry. Hardship allows borrowers in genuine financial hardship to apply to their lenders for additional time to pay arrears. You will also be advised of the dispute-resolution process so you can lodge a dispute if you are not happy with the lender's decision.

&**TIP:** If for any reason you fall into arrears, it's important to understand that the lender will be wanting to talk to you as soon as possible. Avoiding the lender may make the situation worse. Remember to:

1. Communicate with the lender.
2. Get independent advice from a lawyer or accountant.
3. Make a payment, even if it's not the full repayment. This shows the lender you are trying to solve the problem.
4. Don't enter into an agreement to pay a different amount if you know you will not be able to make the payment.
5. Get budgetary assistance.
6. Reduce repayments to interest only.
7. Investigate the possibility of relief from mortgage assistance schemes.
8. Remember, you may be able to access your superannuation on a limited basis to pay arrears.
9. Always check if you qualify for assistance from the lender on the grounds of hardship.

10. Keep a record of all communications you have made and steps you have taken to get out of arrears. These may be critical if the lender takes you to court to repossess your property. Courts will be more likely to give you more time to pay if they see you are genuinely attempting to pay the arrears.

Repossession

The legal process the lender will undertake to repossess the property is controlled by the courts. The process is slightly different in each state, but in general it follows these steps:

1. Notice of demand:

   The lender will issue you a notice of demand. This is a formal notice to the borrowers that legal action to repossess the property is about to start. The document outlines the amount of arrears required to be paid to stop legal action. Generally, you have thirty days to pay the arrears or come to an arrangement to pay the arrears to the lender over time.

   The lender will charge for issuing the notice of demand, which can cost up to $400.

2. Statement of claim:

   If the lender has either not been paid the arrears in full or has not been able to come to an arrangement with you for payment, the lender will issue a statement of claim. This must be personally served on all borrowers, meaning you will be handed the document by a process server. The statement of claim will also be served on anyone living at the property, so if your property is rented, the tenants will be given notice that the lender is taking legal action to repossess the property.

   Even if court proceedings have commenced, you may still be able to lodge a complaint with the lender's dispute resolution scheme. Such a complaint will stop the legal action until it is formally resolved.

3. Court hearing:

   A court hearing will be arranged by the lender's solicitor. The court will review the statement of claim and hear any defence you may lodge. It is very important that you have legal representation at this hearing. If the statement of claim is not defended, the court will find in favour of the lender. The court will then decide whether to award judgement to the lender. If the court does this, a default judgement is approved; this allows the lender to move to the final steps to repossess the property.

4. Writ of possession:

   The lender, having a default judgement, then requests a writ of possession. This court document allows the sheriff to start the eviction process. It usually takes seven to fourteen days to be processed by the courts.

5. Notice to vacate:

   The lender, having received the writ of possession, instructs the sheriff to issue a notice to vacate to anyone living at the property. The sheriff will often nail the notice to the front door of the property. The sheriff will usually undertake the eviction within two weeks of doing this.

6. Eviction and property in possession:

   The sheriff will complete the eviction. If you are still in the property, you will be told to leave. You will not be allowed a delay to remove any personal belongings. The lender will arrange to change the locks on the property and otherwise ensure you have no access to it. The sheriff will call the police if you do not comply with orders.

   The property is now in the lender's possession (property in possession). You must not return to the property. If you do, the lender will call the police and have you removed and potentially arrested. The lender will now prepare the property for sale by making any urgent repairs and completing a general cleaning, including removing any personal belongings you may have left behind.

7. Mortgagee-in-possession sale:

The lender has to sell the property as quickly as possible and is obliged to sell the property for the best possible price by "testing the market". This usually means sale by auction. The lender is obliged to ensure the property is sold for the highest price, not simply for the amount of the outstanding debt. If the lender sells the property for more than you owe, less expenses, you will receive the balance. If, however, the property is sold for a price that does not fully repay the lender, you will still be liable for the remaining debt. The lender can still take further legal action to recover the remaining debt and even put you into bankruptcy.

While the lender will not want to disclose that the property sale is a mortgagee-in-possession sale, the fact is that it will be clear from the sale contracts that the lender is selling the property. As a general rule, properties sold by lenders sell for less than if you were to sell the property yourself. The public sees mortgagee-in-possession sales as an opportunity to get a bargain from a seller that must sell. If you have the opportunity to sell the property yourself, you should consider this, as you may be able to get a better price than the lender. After all, you will have the property furnished and looking its best, but the lender will need to sell an empty property.

It's important to understand that you can repay the arrears at any time up to the day of eviction, and the lender will stop the process. However, lenders holding a default judgement can quickly restart the process if you fall back into arrears.

💥**WARNING:** If you fall into arrears, seek assistance immediately! Get independent advice from a lawyer—don't attempt to avoid the problem. After all, the lender knows where you live!

Chapter 10:

Alternative ways to get onto the property ladder

Purchasing your first home can be very difficult. The government grants available do help, but they often have a limited affect on housing affordability in capital cities, where first-home buyers may receive little or no assistance in paying stamp duty due to the price of the property.

So how can you get into housing without having to save a 20 percent deposit? Remember that if you are in Sydney and purchase a property for $500,000, that deposit is $100,000.

Option 1: The First Home Buyer's Syndicate

Look to purchase a house with someone else. This means you can pool your funds to get a bigger deposit. The repayments are also shared.

This does have drawbacks, as you are only a part owner and you may have a different view on home ownership than your partner. So before you purchase a property, have a written agreement that outlines how much you each own, what maintenance requirements you will each meet, and the process for either of the parties to sell their share of the property.

Option 2: Purchase a Rental Property

You could purchase a rental property. This means you lose the opportunity to access the First Home Owner Grants, but benefits include:

- Interest on your loan will be tax deductible (as will expenses such as rates and insurance)
- As the property is tenanted, you will have income from the property to help pay the loan
- You can buy a cheaper property, even an interstate property
- You will still get capital gains, but you will have to pay capital gains tax

Option 3: The Fixer-Upper

This is the old trick of buying the worst house on the street and slowly renovating it. However, this can mean living in a hovel for a long time and maxing out your credit cards just to have running water!

Option 4: Boarders

If you need extra income to afford the loan, you may be able to use income from boarders to assist. It may be just enough to get you the loan.

Option 5: Family Assistance

Can you buy the property with the assistance of a family member? This may mean siblings buying and living together, or parents offering a guarantee to reduce the reliance on LMI. As with buying in a syndicate, always have an agreement in writing so everyone is protected.

Option 6: An Equity Finance Mortgage (EFM)

An EFM works in conjunction with a traditional home loan. Together they let you move some of the expense of a traditional home loan to a later time when you eventually sell your property. The EFM allows you to borrow up to 20 percent of the property's value as an interest-free loan. You are not required to make any monthly interest repayments throughout the term of the EFM loan, which you can hold for up to twenty-five years. Instead, when you sell the property or repay the EFM for some other reason, you repay the EFM amount you originally borrowed plus up to a 40 percent share of any increase in the value of the property (assuming you take out a 20 percent EFM).

The obvious benefit is that you can get into housing quickly and usually purchase a better quality home. The disadvantage is if your property values dramatically increase, you will pass over a potentially huge amount of money to the EFM lender. There are also issues around renovations and improvements you make, which can result in ongoing revaluation fees.

Option 7: State Housing Programs/Private Housing Programs

In SA and WA, the state governments offer lending programs to assist people into housing. This is not just for low-income earners; the programs also offer high LVR loans to young professionals.

There are some private charitable organisations (such as Habitat for Humanity) that assist people by providing either discounted loans or discounted houses.

Option 8: Invest in Overseas Property

You could purchase a rental property overseas. This means you don't lose the opportunity to access the First Home Owner Grants later. Also, some overseas investments can be much cheaper. For example, in New Zealand there is no stamp duty and no capital gains tax.

👍PROS

- Interest on your loan will be tax deductible (as will expenses such as rates and insurance)
- As the property is tenanted, you will have rent income to help pay the loan
- You can buy a cheaper property (you may even be able to benefit from a stronger Australian dollar)

- Tax benefits (such as no capital gains or stamp duty)
- Australian tax benefits (for example, the cost of an annual site visit being tax deductible)

☞ CONS

- Exchange rate risk: you are exposed to fluctuations in the exchange rate
- May be difficult to manage from a distance
- You will most likely not have a detailed knowledge of the local property market

Option 9: Employer-Provided Housing Benefits

Some occupations, such as the Australian armed forces, offer subsidies to assist staff in paying a home loan. Some mining companies offer subsidies to assist employees who build homes in settlements close to mines.

Option 10: Move Outside of the Capital Cities

Are you sick of the rat race? Could you live in a small town? Then moving to country Australia could be for you. House prices in country Australia are about half the cost of housing in capital cities. NSW has even offered a grant of $7,000 to assist families to move out of Sydney, Newcastle, and Wollongong. But lenders view country Australia as less desirable. Houses take longer to sell and sell for less, so you may still have to find a 20 percent deposit. However, when housing is priced around $250,000, this is a deposit $50,000 less than in the capital cities.

SUMMARY: There are a lot of ways onto the property ladder. You don't have to limit yourself to saving a huge deposit or taking out a 97 percent loan. Be creative and you can find alternatives!

Chapter 11:

Conclusion

I f I was looking for a new loan, I know I wouldn't have a lot of time to speak to lenders, so I would use a mortgage broker. The key would be finding a mortgage broker I could trust and work with.

Your mortgage broker has to work for you and the lender at the same time. A good mortgage broker will be knowledgeable and understand the lending market and your needs as a borrower. Mortgage brokers have software to help you locate the appropriate loan from a list of potentially hundreds of lenders. This can save you huge amounts of time by only listing loans that meet your basic needs.

✐**TIP:** Top ten tips for getting a home loan:

1. Take advantage of the services of a mortgage broker.
2. Confirm how much you really need to borrow.
3. Save more so you have to borrow less.
4. Increase your income and decrease your existing debt. This will increase the maximum loan you can get.
5. Close unwanted credit cards or store cards. Again, this will increase the maximum loan you can get.
6. Keep a clean credit history and know what's in your credit file.

7. Don't apply at every lender.

8. Have all the required information with you when you talk to your mortgage broker. Before you get together, ask what you should bring.

9. Understand what features you need and what you are paying for them. Don't forget to negotiate fees!

10. Ask questions. Why does the recommended loan meet your needs?

If you find yourself in arrears, it's important you get independent advice from a lawyer immediately. There are a number of options, but it's important to look at your options as quickly as possible.

Throughout the book I have attempted to answer some very important questions:

1. Should you do a do-it-yourself (DIY) search or use a mortgage broker to find your next home loan?

    Clearly, a DIY search is not as beneficial as going to a mortgage broker. While you should look first at your existing lender, having more options provided by an independent and knowledgeable specialist is a good idea.

2. How do you get approved quickly and without hassles?

    Make sure you know what you want, have all the information and documents on hand, and provide clear time frames for when you expect an answer.

3. What loan should you get? This includes looking at variable rate vs. fixed rate options.

    I personally believe variable rate full-featured loans offer the best mix of price and flexibility. A 100 percent offset account offers you the opportunity to reduce interest costs while having access to extra money when you need it.

If you are rate-sensitive, or if you want to reduce the risk of variable rate increases, then splitting your loan into part fixed and part variable is a good idea. Personally, I don't believe fixed rates in the longer terms—five or more years—are a good idea, as the risk of the rate becoming higher than the variable rate is more likely.

The Australian home loan market is very competitive and offers you a wide range of choices. To take full advantage, you need to understand not only the offers but the lending policies, and for that you should use a mortgage broker.

Ask your friends or family members if they have used a mortgage broker and can recommend a good contact. The lending industry is still growing, and the lenders want your business. There are good deals out there. Good luck on your search!

💣**WARNING:** The information in this book is provided "as-is," without warranty of any kind. I do not warrant that the information is accurate, up-to-date, or compliant with any Australian state or federal legislation. The information is of a general nature, and I strongly recommend readers seek independent legal and financial advice prior to entering into any financial arrangement.

About The Author

∙∙∙

Andrew Brien has over eighteen years' experience in banking and finance in both Australia and New Zealand. He has held senior roles in banks (operations manager at ING Bank) and non-bank lenders (projects and product development manager at Australia's biggest non-bank residential lender). He is currently a senior manager in a loan-servicing provider based in NSW.

If you would like to ask the author any questions (please, no requests for legal or financial advice), you can visit the Loan Arranger on the web at: www.loanarrangerguide.com.au or e-mail your question to questions@loanarrangerguide.com.au.

Index